S0-BSH-597

Continued Praise for ...*the Best Policy*

"This book speaks to the importance of providing for families and their needs through the effective use of Life Insurance Trusts. Tate's book makes a very complicated subject understandable, and he provides real-life examples of how his management of irrevocable life insurance trusts has made a difference in the lives of families who have benefited from his trusted services. The Groome family has been providing critical life insurance solutions to our family and our business for three generations. Their comprehensive life insurance planning and management has proven to be invaluable to our family.

I am delighted that Tate has been able to document the wealth of experience and extensive learning that his family has accumulated over decades to produce this book, which will no doubt serve as a significant source of education for many."

—DIANA "DINI" CECIL PICKERING, Great-Granddaughter of George W. Vanderbilt. Dini is Vice Chairperson of the Board of Directors for The Biltmore Company, which owns and operates Biltmore in Asheville, NC. Biltmore is the private estate of the late George W. Vanderbilt. Dini serves as the Family Office Director and oversees family business initiatives such as family planning meetings and training for future generations. She is also Chairperson of Biltmore's Corporate Philanthropy program. Dini is a sought-after speaker on the topic of family business, having presented for numerous conferences and board meetings.

"This is a very human book, and the best book on life insurance and ILITs that I have read. It's worth reading several times over. I highly recommend it!"

—MICHAEL D. WEINBERG, JD, AEP©, President, The Weinberg Group, Inc.

"I sat down and read Tate's book this morning, and it is excellent! Tate made a complex subject accessible and enjoyable with all of the wonderful and heartfelt stories. I desperately wish I had read this book 25 years ago, when we were putting together my mother's irrevocable life insurance trust. I was young, did not understand what was happening, and did not even know what questions to ask. Unfortunately, the attorney made some mistakes with the Crummey notices, which later caused us great stress and expense. Had I read ...*the Best Policy* I would have been able to avoid all of that frustration and pain. If you're involved in any way with life insurance, you absolutely need to read this book (and give it to your clients)."

—JOHN SPENCE, one of the top 100 business thought leaders in America in the area of trustworthy business behavior

---

"Our century-old business chartered a private trust company in 2012 to support the continued longevity of our family enterprise. That trust company has become responsible for a number of irrevocable life insurance trusts.

This book by Tate Groome is a superb and timely contribution to the growing knowledge requirements of both our Board of Directors and the operating leadership of our trust organization. I am grateful to the author for this effort to bring clarity to the issues surrounding the obligations we have taken on in our quest to build our family company."

—JIM ETHIER, Chairman of the Board, Bush Brothers & Company

"I was thrilled to see that a book about insurance could be so informative, while simultaneously being so entertaining! Tate has done a great job merging the human element with technical data in this publication. It is a book that fiduciaries managing ILITs, as well as grantors & beneficiaries of trusts should read."

—BECKY T. KELLY, Managing Partner, Fiduciary Education Center, LLC

"Tate Groome's book, ...*the Best Policy*, zeros in on what professionals in the life insurance industry have long known: 'the process of designing and managing policies on an ongoing basis is a far more important decision than trying to pick the best policy.' Tate's book strikes an interesting balance in showing how life insurance policies work best. It requires both the specialized knowledge of these complex and opaque financial products and, with a product that is designed by its nature to span generations, the ongoing care for clients. The mix of personal stories and technical information in the book shows how this has played out over the last 65 years at Tate's firm, Colton Groome."

—LAWRENCE J. RYBKA JD, CFP®, President & CEO, ValMark Securities. ValMark Securities is a specialty broker-dealer that supports 120 carefully selected member firms like Colton Groome nationwide. ValMark has, in the last 52 years through its combined buying power, helped its member firms place over 20 billion dollars of face amount with two dozen insurance companies. Larry is also the author of dozens of published articles on life insurance including the award-winning articles: "A Case for Variable Life," "Whose Policy is it Anyway," and "Insurance Policy Selection For Irrevocable Life Insurance Trusts: New Challenges For Trustees And Advisors."

"This book connects the dots for everyone who is concerned (or advising those concerned) about their family, their wealth, and legacy. Tate's writing is not only very accessible, but also enables anyone to understand how the mindful use of insurance can be a vital tool to achieving your goals, family harmony, and planning that aligns with your values."

—DR. GREG MCCANN, Founder of McCann & Associates, Founder of Stetson University's Family Enterprise Center

---

"This thoughtful and well-organized book marks a new generation of resources for family businesses. Tate's experience in the field of life insurance is evident in his writing. He has woven the personal stories of his clients together beautifully to explain the concepts. It read more like a conversation over coffee rather than a lumbering book of insurance information. He not only understands the complicated issues, but has the ability to explain it in simple, unassuming prose. Tate is a real pro, working with his father and brother in the family business that has served the area for over fifty years. Tate's consideration and appreciation for family bonds leaps off the pages of this book, and his encouragements will inspire you to design your legacy, starting today!"

—CINDY CLARKE is the Executive Director of the University of North Carolina Asheville Family Business Forum since 2006. The Forum is a continuing education series designed to support family businesses and was established in 2001.

"In my work with business families I encounter the whole range of human emotions. Often I am referred by trusted advisors with clients who know what needs to be done, but who are resistant to dealing with mortality issues. One in 3 family businesses will pass successfully to the next generation of owners. Many of those that fail do so because of liquidity crises at the time of death of the owner. Nothing fills that gap quite like life insurance. Tate talks about the 'dreaded' subject with humor and insight. His personal stories add a depth to his writing that is often missing in technical books."

—ROBERT CALDWELL is the founder of Family Firm Resources LLC of Charlotte. He regularly consults with, speaks and teaches on the subject the human side of family owned business. Since 2001, Robert has been the Babcock Family Business Fellow in the Wake Forest University Schools of Business.

"Being in the financial services business for 40 years, I've read a ton of books. Tate Groome is so passionate about his message I knew the book would be awesome and I was correct. My interest was piqued instantly quickly as I read ...*the Best Policy: Irrevocable Life Insurance Trusts: Getting to the Heart of the Matter.* Having a story weaved into how important life insurance can be allows you to experience it through someone else's eyes. Tate did a great job of clarifying his message to the reader while keeping them intrigued until the end. A must-read coming from someone that has written 8 books and understands how important education helps people. A must-read for all!!!"

—GINA PELLEGRINI, Owner of Pellegrini Team Consulting & Strategic Coach® Coach

"Tate has demystified life insurance in a way that is practical and useful, yet insightful. His insights and experience will greatly assist you as you navigate the process."

—PATRICIA M. ANNINO Esquire. Patricia is the leading authority on how women can create, grow and keep their wealth. Ms. Annino is a nationally recognized authority on estate planning and taxation, serving the estate planning needs of families, individuals, and owners of closely held businesses. She is the author of a number of books, including *Cracking the $$ Code, What Successful Men Know and You Don't (Yet!), Women in Family Business: What Keeps You Up at Night?* and *Women & Money: A Practical Guide to Estate Planning.*

"In reading ...*the Best Policy* I was struck by the thoughtful stories that made the financial products understandable to not only professionals in the field but understandable to me and to the families I work with who must make the ultimate and educated decision of what to have in place when they are no longer here. Never an easy discussion but one that must be had and revisited periodically as the years pass. I met Tate and his family years ago and I am continually impressed at their dedication to improving the knowledge base and processes available to their clients, the industry and complex families of wealth everywhere."

—ANN DUGAN is a 4th generation member of a business owning family, founder of the Institute for Entrepreneurial Excellence at the University of Pittsburgh and currently a managing director of family business services with HeadwatersSC in Sewickley, Pennsylvania

About the Book

We're all familiar with the old adage: "Honesty is the best policy." The adage drove our ethics as children, and all too often, we lose sight of the best policy as adults. In *...the Best Policy*, G. Tate Groome works to guide fiduciaries to the irrevocable life insurance policy structure that is truly right for their clients, deftly combining insurance expertise acquired over three generations with honesty and a code of conduct in an otherwise sterile business world. With a gentle emphasis on the personal, loving element that lies behind each policy, Groome uses *...the Best Policy* to help grantors and fiduciaries alike understand effective methods to monitor, manage, and sometimes restructure ILITs so that each grantor and trust beneficiary can have the *best* policy indeed.

...the
Best Policy

Irrevocable Life Insurance Trusts:
Getting to the Heart of the Matter

G. TATE GROOME, CFP®, CLU®

LIFETRUST3D, LLC
Asheville, NC

Copyright © 2015 by G. Tate Groome, CFP®, CLU®

All Rights Reserved.

No part of this book may be reproduced, stored in a retrieval system or transmitted in any form by an electronic, mechanical, photocopying, recording means or otherwise without prior written permission of the publisher.

For more information contact:
LifeTrust3D, LLC
1127 B-Hendersonville Rd.
Asheville, NC 28803
www.tategroome.com

Paperback: 978-0-692-37354-5
eBook: 978-0-692-37355-2

Library of Congress Control Number: 2015931658

CONTENTS

Preface: The Challenge

I GET IT. I'm fighting an uphill battle in wanting you to read a book about trust-owned life insurance. You probably don't love it like I do, or grew up immersed in it like I did. But I like a good challenge! The thing is—this is not really a book about life insurance. It's a book about people who love people, and their desire to protect their loved ones.

So who's this book for, anyway? Well, if you're reading this book, know that it's for *you.*

It is for you, the trust officer—whether you're seasoned or fresh out of school and looking for a way to better understand the challenges and rewards of working in the world of Irrevocable Life Insurance Trust. It is for you, the estate planning attorney, accountant, or wealth advisor who preaches to clients that planning is not a one-time event; it is dynamic and ever-changing.

It is for you, the Chief Financial Officer, Treasurer, Board Member, or other fiduciary serving single-family or multi-family offices, and it is for those family offices that work hard to manage the life insurance portfolios of the families they support, and simply to communicate to those families the dynamic nature of those portfolios. This is a book I hope you'll pass on to your clients—be they trust grantors or trust beneficiaries—to reinforce the impact your work and planning has on families and legacies. It is for the non-professional trustee: the brother, parent, aunt, or family friend who has agreed to be a trustee and needs to ensure effective administration and monitoring of an unfamiliar product. And finally, it is for the grantors—you, the trust creators. You spend time, money, and sometimes heartache and tears creating a vehicle that can deliver your lifetime's work, savings, wealth, and values to the children and grandchildren you love so dearly. Your plan is unlike anyone else's in the world. You entrust life insurance advisors, life insurance companies, trustees, and your other advisors to ensure that your plan blossoms. This book is for you.

I guarantee that if you don't catch yourself nodding (in agreement, not off to sleep), smiling (at least a little smirk), appreciating life insurance (even just a little bit more than you do now), or thinking of a client or friend who needs to read this, you can e-mail <u>discover@ LifeTrust3D.com</u> and I will refund your money. Deal? Okay—let's do this!

1

Origins

MY JOURNEY IN the life insurance industry actually began on Halloween night in 1960. (Stay with me, now—I was born in 1979, but my story began before my parents even dreamed me up.) My then eight-year-old father, George, was out trick-or-treating when he spotted another young boy in a ghost costume. The "ghost" kept tripping over the hem of his costume—and candy went flying everywhere. George stopped his trick-or-treating, helped the boy to his feet, collected his candy, and then they went on together to the next house. Despite George's efforts, his new friend kept falling. After the fourth time the ghost tripped, George finally asked the other boy his name. "Walter," the ghost said, grateful that George continued to help him while the other kids just passed him by.

Little did young George know that his small act of kindness that Halloween night would change his life—and the ripple effect it produced would influence mine. Young George Groome and Walter Colton quickly became lifelong friends. Once brought together, the two were inseparable. They remained friends through adulthood, rooming together during college at the University of North Carolina at Chapel Hill. (Go Heels!)

My father's story is a riches-to-rags, then back to riches story. George was the youngest of five children, and his father, W.J., had a dream job at the Pepsi Cola Bottling Company. When my father was eight, W.J. lost his job at Pepsi. Serendipitously, George met young Walter around the same time, and he started spending a lot of his time at the Colton house.

As the youngest of five children, young George's life was very different from the lives of his older siblings. Reluctant to talk about his childhood, my father often jokes that he spent so much time at the Coltons' because he just liked hanging out with Walter's three sisters! He doesn't mention the mansion he grew up in before they lost everything, or the two full-time housekeepers who worked there. He doesn't like to tell us about having to work at a local factory during high school, sweeping glass on the night shifts, so that he could help support their household. He doesn't talk about the many nights he spent at the laundromat with his mom, or the time he stood up to his father during one of W.J.'s alcohol-induced rages. Although I can't blame him for loving the Colton girls as a teenager, I know the real reason he spent so much time there was because they made him feel like family.

Tradition was important to the Colton family, and in keeping with tradition they always went to Henry Colton's office on the fifteenth floor of the BB&T building in downtown Asheville to watch the Christmas parade. Being part of the family, George was always included. During Thanksgiving of 1972, as my father was nearing the end of his college career at UNC Business School, that tradition of watching the Christmas parade turned into much more. When the parade ended, everyone went their own way except for George and Henry, who sat quietly gazing over downtown and the beautiful Blue Ridge Mountains beyond it. George said to Henry, "I don't know exactly what you do, Mr. Colton, but I know it has something to do with finance. I know you're well respected and successful, and that you always seem to have a smile on your face. I want to be just like you. Can I come work with you after graduation?"

With his own son Walter pursuing a career in international business, Henry had already been considering hiring George to help continue the family business.

George, a brilliant student, was highly qualified, and Henry knew he could count on him to do the job right. The two looked at each other thoughtfully, and after a moment, Henry said, "Of course."

That first chance encounter over trick-or-treating led to my father dedicating his life to the wealth management and protection industry. George went to work for Mr. Colton after his final exam, and the company began to evolve into the incredible organization that it is today. The name of the firm today, Colton Groome & Company, pays homage to the man who first planted the seed for my father's career ... and for mine.

Henry's impact on my father's life shaped *my* life before I even understood how important it truly was. Before I was drawn to my father's career, I followed in my mother's footsteps, becoming a teacher in the inner-city school system after graduating from college. I started in an at-risk elementary school where I coached the middle school basketball team. I loved the impact I was able to make in other people's lives.

However, I eventually realized how badly I wanted to learn about the business world, and who better to teach me than my father, the very best man—and professional—I felt I'd ever been around? He was in the prime of his career at the time, and I realized what a rare opportunity I had to learn from someone so experienced and educated. My other option, of course, would have been to go back to school for business, but I felt (and still feel) that a person can get a master's degree from an educational institution or a Ph.D. in life experience. I chose the latter, and from then on I attended the "George Groome School of Business" every day.

So many businesspeople of my generation want to be investment managers. After observing and working with my father, I knew I didn't want to manage money like everyone else. I wanted to protect families. I wanted to protect legacies, not just for today, but for generations to come. That's why life insurance is the only industry for me.

From L to R: Tate Groome, Matt Groome, Henry Colton, George Groome

2

How $22 Million Changed My Life... Not Just the Beneficiary's

"EVERYONE WAS LAUGHING," Charles said to me. I waited.

Charles, a former real estate developer, had already purchased a $10 million Whole Life insurance policy years ago. Charles was a family friend and a client of ours, but I knew his situation had changed. I called him one morning when he had just returned from a family vacation and asked if I could meet with him. He replied, "How soon can you be at my office?"

Puzzled by how quickly he suddenly wanted to meet with me, I told him I'd be there in fifteen minutes. I scrambled to prepare for our meeting and rushed across town to his office. I knew Charles well enough to know that if he wanted to meet, he wanted to meet right then and you'd better be there!

Charles had accumulated significant debt on a large real estate project. The project would eventually turn out to be quite profitable, but I knew he needed to increase his life insurance. His initial goal had been to make sure that his family didn't inherit his debt and that they would always be able to maintain their standard of living, even if he wasn't there as the provider. However, the stakes had recently increased with this particular project.

As I sank into the deep, brown, leather chair in his boardroom, Charles said again, "Everyone was laughing." He smiled, and I smiled with him. "I want to make sure that my family can always keep laughing," he continued. "I believe I'm now ready to purchase the additional $10 million life insurance policy that you've been recommending." Based on some of his desires and his specific situation, Charles had decided long ago that owning life insurance inside an irrevocable trust wasn't right for him, and he held firm on his decision. Even so, I sat in that brown chair for almost two hours that day, and together we designed *his* insurance plan: one that would meet his goals and needs both today and for his lifetime.

Charles was happily married with an adult daughter and four grandchildren. He owned a beautiful home on the Outer Banks in North Carolina, and he'd just returned from taking the whole family to the beach for a week. He told me about the perfect ocean breeze and the soothing sound of the waves washing up on the shore. Seated in a beach chair, he'd held his wife's hands and watched his daughter basking in the sunshine while he himself basked in the sheer joy of the experience and listened to the laughter of his grandchildren. "I closed my eyes and heard my grandkids laugh," he told me, "and I just never want to worry that they won't laugh again."

A life insurance policy can be an intimidating investment, one that clients—especially younger clients—don't often like to think about. To so many, thinking about "life insurance" is akin to thinking about "what happens when I die," and let's be honest—most people don't really want to think about that. I watched my client's eyes light up every time he mentioned his grandchildren, and it was then that I truly realized that a life insurance policy isn't just a "policy"; it is a reflection of the love one has for his or her family. Charles was the quintessential patriarch, a self-made man who wanted nothing more than to provide for his family, even in death. I wanted to help him do that.

Money doesn't necessarily provide happiness, but it will absolutely allow for certain freedoms. Clients buy life insurance because they love their families. Whether it's the oldest member of the family or a newly married couple wanting to make sure they can take care of their loved ones, the biggest motivator to purchase life insurance stems from love. In so many words, Charles told me something I hear most of my clients say: "I love my family, and one of the best ways I can take care of them is to look out for everyone financially. And one of the best ways I can do that is to ensure that they won't have to take on my debts, and that a reliable reserve is here for them."

One of the biggest conundrums with *any* life insurance portfolio lies in balancing premiums and current finances with the ultimate value of the policy. An issue to date is that many people purchased policies back in the late 80s and 90s, when the estate tax exemption was significantly lower than it is today. A lot can change for a family in ten or twenty years, though, and perhaps they're finding now that they don't need as much life insurance, or they need additional coverage, or they no longer can afford

> People often think that life insurance is a very static financial vehicle, but nothing could be farther from the truth.... All life insurance is incredibly dynamic, with many moving parts, and it has to be managed that way.

that same premium that may have been a drop in the bucket before. Maybe their goals have simply changed, or perhaps the beneficiaries need access to some of the cash value for emergencies. Anything can shift, and it's crucial to make sure that clients can fund their premiums and that their life insurance policies make sense. People often think that life insurance is a very static financial vehicle, but nothing could be farther from the truth. And owning life insurance inside an irrevocable trust adds yet another layer of complication—as if life insurance weren't already complex enough. All life insurance is incredibly dynamic, with many moving parts, and it has to be managed that way.

Life changes. Economic times change. Political environments and tax laws change. Insurance performance and products change. Change is inevitable. The policy that best serves a client needs to be properly structured and managed while still allowing for change.

To create the *best* policy for a client, we have to go back and ask the question that we so often asked as children: *why?* Why did we buy life insurance in the first place? Why do we maintain it? In order to effectively manage your clients' life insurance policies, take a step back. Start with *why*, and keep asking as time passes. "Why are you purchasing a life insurance policy?" you

> To effectively manage your clients' life insurance policies, take a step back.... Sometimes the goal is simply to reduce risk for a policy that's not performing well or could lapse. Life insurance is all part of a bigger plan, and it must be consistently reevaluated as life changes.

might ask a client. "What are your goals for your policy *today*—to protect your wealth or protect yourself from debt? To provide an inheritance? To leverage your existing assets? To minimize tax implications? To provide for your favorite charity? How do we make the most efficient use of your assets? How can we maximize benefit for the trust and for the trust beneficiaries?" Sometimes the goal is simply to reduce risk for a policy that's not performing well or could lapse. Life insurance is all part of a bigger plan, and it must be consistently reevaluated as life changes.

Have you ever heard of the classic Chinese Bamboo Tree parable? I learned it just this year from a church sermon:

You take a little seed, plant it, water it, and fertilize it for a whole year—and nothing happens.

You water and fertilize the seed for a second year. Nothing.

A third year of you caring for the plant passes—nothing. You water and fertilize for a fourth year—*still* nothing.

You water and fertilize for a fifth year. Sometime during the fifth year, finally, gratifyingly, the Chinese bamboo tree sprouts ... and grows ninety feet in ninety days!

Nourishing and reaping the benefits of a trust-owned life insurance policy is surprisingly similar to the story of the Chinese bamboo tree. During those five years, you don't necessarily see any progress above ground, but the root system is establishing itself as a solid foundation for the future. Over the course of five years, it spreads and deepens in preparation for the dramatic growth ahead—and when it is finally time, the beautiful plant that you expected to see sprouting slowly from the ground surpasses expectations because it was cared for properly.

Many consumers feel like the purchase of life insurance is the ultimate goal, and that once they've purchased it, it will take care of itself. They work and work, trying to find *the* right policy, going through underwriting and jumping through all the various hoops necessary to purchasing a policy—and it gets even more complicated when the policy is purchased within a trust. Once consumers find and buy that policy, they think, *That's it. I'm done. I've taken care of the work, and I don't need to do anything else.*

I learned from my father that the purchase is not in fact the end game—it's just the beginning. The policy has to be nurtured for a long, long time. We need to make sure that the roots are established and strong, and we need to pay attention to environmental changes so we know when we're watering it too much or not fertilizing enough (i.e., putting too much premium in or not funding the policy enough).

The ultimate benefits to life insurance are numerous: estate planning, charitable giving, family protection, business succession, inheritance—the list goes on. The real key to owning a policy, though, is monitoring and managing what you have so that you and the beneficiaries *can* reap those benefits. A homeowner can't buy a house and then never do any repairs or adjustments. In the same way, a client shouldn't invest in a policy and then never adjust. After an agent sells a policy, there technically is no contractual obligation on his or her part to manage it; they've received their commission and are ready to move on. Almost a third of trust-owned policies are left unmanaged. (And keep in mind that these are the wealthiest of Americans, who presumably have access to the best resources available!)

Leaving a policy unmanaged is like leaving your Chinese bamboo tree without nourishment. You can't reap the benefits if you don't help to create and maintain the foundation.

> Leaving a policy unmanaged is like leaving your Chinese bamboo tree without nourishment. You can't reap the benefits if you don't help to create and maintain the foundation.

Remember my client Charles? As a fresh-faced twenty-something, I was surprised when he trusted me enough to go beyond our typical client-advisor relationship and confide in me. Charles was a big, intimidating man even in his later years; he *looked* like a powerful businessman. I certainly didn't anticipate that he would put such faith in a young guy like me, much less that he would purchase millions of dollars worth of life insurance from me. But I spent more time than I had expected to in his office, developing a deep relationship that lasted. I learned of his greatest joys and sorrows, his fears, his relationship with his father—all intimacies that I'd never expected (nor thought I deserved) to receive.

Charles was an excellent judge of character, and he saw something in me that allowed him to trust me deeply, and that trust allowed me to move forward confidently in my career. I felt that if Charles trusted me, then I didn't have to be intimated to approach anyone. This is a gift for which I will be forever grateful.

After Charles and I had been working for some time to re-engineer his insurance plan, I realized that we would be able to reduce his six-figure premium while simultaneously increasing the death benefit. This was in the day when almost any well-funded Whole Life contract could be exchanged for Universal Life with secondary guarantees, an eliminated or reduced premium, and increased death benefits. Oh, the good old days! If you are in the insurance business, you know such contracts are few and far between in today's environment. Reducing his premium allowed Charles to focus on the real estate debt that had been weighing on him.

Sadly, Charles passed away too soon, only three years after we increased his life insurance—but the seed that we planted and nourished together sprouted during those three years. I'd never wish death before its time on anyone, but I know that being prepared gave Charles comfort.

Shortly after Charles's death, I knocked on his daughter Hillary's door. She opened it and greeted me warmly as her kids chased each other in the hallway behind her. I gave her a big hug and then handed her an envelope. As a single mother, Hillary had been supporting her children on her own, and fortunately Charles had been able to assist her during his lifetime. At my initial meetings with Charles, as I sat in that brown leather chair, he had explained to me that Hillary would need financial help if he wasn't here to support her. Together, Charles and I had come up with a solution.

Hillary eyed the envelope curiously, then looked back at me. I nodded encouragingly, and she slowly opened the envelope. She pulled out the enclosed paper and stared, first in disbelief and then in shock, at a check for $2 million made out in her name.

Charles's widow was the beneficiary of the first $20,000,000. Charles and I had designed his policy this way largely to pay off his real estate debt. Our intention was also to provide income for the next thirty-plus years so the love of his life could live comfortably, the way she would have were her husband still living. With some thoughtful and careful life insurance plan design, though, Charles and I were able to increase the death benefit from $20,000,000 to $22,000,000 so that there was an extra $2,000,000 available for Hillary.

Check in hand, an astonished Hillary looked back up at me—and burst into tears. Hillary had been under the impression that her father's life insurance would be used primarily to pay off his debt and benefit her mother, and she'd had no idea that anything significant was coming to her. "You don't know what this means to me," she told me through her sobs of relief. "You do not know what this means to me."

That extra $2 million made a world of difference for Hillary. It allowed her to care for her family in the way that she so badly wanted to and in the manner that Charles had imagined. I have learned in my career that money—or more specifically, life insurance proceeds— gives families and beneficiaries financial freedom at the time when they most desperately need it.

Sitting with Hillary as she wept changed me. It was a weighty but gratifying moment in my career, and that moment has stayed with me. It was on that day that I saw how much difference a life insurance policy could make. After surviving grief and loss, a beneficiary can be handed the smallest piece of paper and know, without a doubt, that they were loved.

Charles was a real estate developer, so liquidity was vital to his business, and he had determined early on that he didn't want a trust to own his life insurance or the cash value that he'd accumulated within the policies. However, an irrevocable trust is an incredibly powerful planning tool that, when managed correctly, can cement one's legacy for years to come. Had we made the decision to utilize one, we likely could have made postmortem planning for Charles's surviving spouse less complex. Charles lacked a complex understanding of sophisticated planning, though, and his wishes were important to me. As my father always says, "Money in times of no agreements is better than agreements in times of no money." In other words, it was better in this situation to let him do what he felt was best, because pushing him toward a planning technique he wasn't comfortable with might have jeopardized his having life insurance at all.

Now, almost five years after Charles's passing, I often wonder how the ripple effect of his life insurance proceeds will continue to affect his loved ones for generations to come. Charles's family and I have been able to maintain a warm and caring relationship—I see his wife often, and I see Hillary and her children frequently as well. They're all still laughing, and I know Charles hears them.

3

The Irrevocable Life Insurance Trust: A Practical Overview

THE IRREVOCABLE LIFE insurance trust (or ILIT) is one of the most powerful estate planning tools ever created. When managed correctly, this incredibly potent tool can secure one's legacy for years to come. However, ILITs are often undermanaged and overlooked. While many believe an ILIT owning life insurance is a static wealth transfer vehicle, that notion cannot be farther from the truth. Both ILITs and the life insurance policies they own are incredibly dynamic and need to be managed accordingly. The word "irrevocable" intimidates some (like Charles), but the true meaning behind it is simply that the terms of the trust generally can't be changed by the grantor (the creator of the trust). *Changed*, however, is very different in this context from *managed*, and by investing in a trust and maintaining it properly, a client can benefit greatly.

Again, people purchase life insurance because they care about their families. By utilizing a properly structured ILIT, grantors can leverage their trust and purchase a significant asset without it being subject to estate taxes, thereby providing the necessary liquidity for their loved ones at death. The grantor of the irrevocable trust transfers to that trust his or her interest in an insurance policy on his or her life. The beneficiaries are notified of the gift and given the right to make a withdrawal of the gift within the time period specified in the trust document (usually thirty days). The expectation is that they will not exercise their right of withdrawal (called Crummey powers). Thereafter, the donor makes annual contributions to the trust, and those contributions are used to pay the premiums on the policy.

In 2015, with the federal estate tax exemption at $5,430,000, many wonder if their ILIT is still applicable.

> By utilizing a properly structured ILIT, grantors can leverage their trust and purchase a significant asset without it being subject to estate taxes, thereby providing the necessary liquidity for their loved ones.

I say yes, yes, and yes again! Ask clients again: why was the policy purchased in the first place? It wasn't solely for estate tax purposes. It was because our clients love the family farm or business, their children, and their grandchildren. Values can be embedded within the provisions of the trust so that it can become an extension of the grantor. Aside from estate and legacy planning, ILITs may also help protect assets from divorce, undue influence, bad decisions, and creditors. Due to more progressive trust laws that include "dynasty" language, certain states such as Alaska, Nevada, South Dakota, and Delaware offer favorable trust provisions that may allow the grantor greater asset protection, and flexibility, and may enable wealth to be protected for future generations.

Each ILIT is unique and should be customized to the grantor's goals. The key to using an irrevocable life insurance trust to a client's advantage lies in managing the trust and its assets prudently. We encourage clients to review their trust documents routinely, along with the assets owned in the trust, in order to be certain that both the document and the assets continue to meet the family's goals.

THE IRREVOCABLE LIFE INSURANCE TRUST

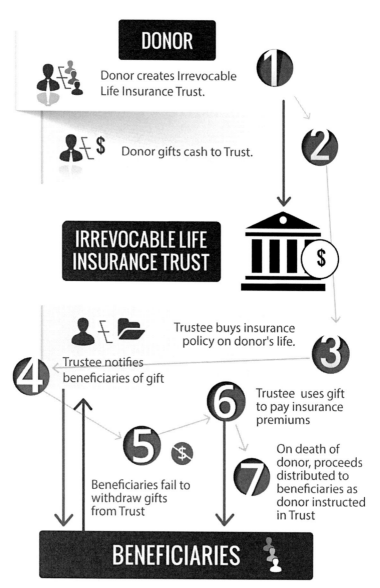

DONOR

Donor creates Irrevocable Life Insurance Trust.

Donor gifts cash to Trust.

IRREVOCABLE LIFE INSURANCE TRUST

Trustee buys insurance policy on donor's life.

Trustee notifies beneficiaries of gift

Trustee uses gift to pay insurance premiums

On death of donor, proceeds distributed to beneficiaries as donor instructed in Trust

Beneficiaries fail to withdraw gifts from Trust

BENEFICIARIES

4

Insurance Design with a Purpose: Matching Your Life Insurance to Your Needs as They Change (and they will!)

JANET, A SWEET, vibrant lady in her seventies, marched into her trust officer's office in frustration. She was recently divorced, in great health, and lived an active lifestyle in her house down by the beach. However, because of her divorce, the assets that she had been living on were dwindling. Her trust-owned life insurance policy had been previously set up so that she was making a gift of $60,000 to the trust each year. The $5 million death benefit was intended to provide for her two adult children and her grandchildren.

Janet loved her children and their families very, very much, but over time, the annual $60,000 contribution became difficult for her to maintain. She'd always been very wealthy, and had been particularly well off when she purchased her policy twenty years earlier. At the time, a $60,000 premium was realistic. The trust officer explained to me that she was living off of the rent she collected from her commercial real estate properties. As much as she didn't want to admit it, she could no longer handle such a substantial premium, as commercial rents had suffered greatly during the real estate crash.

As the trust officer told me the story, what shocked me was that no one had stopped to ask her—*since 1998*—if the $60,000 premium suited her lifestyle as it changed over the years. The insurance company was strong and reliable, and the trust-owned policy was performing very well, but no one had ever asked her if the annual gift was still comfortable. As the grantor of the trust, she didn't receive correspondence from the insurance carrier and didn't quite understand how the trust worked, but she was reluctant to bring it up in conversation because she was uncomfortable no longer being, in her mind, financially self-sufficient.

Janet's insurance policy had accumulated over $1 million in cash value, and in completing our firm's trademarked process, we were able to produce a report for the trustee that could enhance the delivery value of the insurance program significantly. By instituting a prudent and independent process, we were able to utilize the accumulated policy cash value to exchange the existing trust-owned policies for two new ones that better helped both Janet and the trust meet their goals of providing the maximum possible benefit to the trust beneficiaries— her beloved children. We helped her secure a death benefit of $5.2 million instead of the original $5 million, and we were also able to eliminate her annual premium so that she could live her life more comfortably. She was thrilled that she'd be able to leave behind an additional $200,000 for her kids, *plus* whatever assets she could put aside from her previous $60,000 premium.

After I delivered the new policies to the trust officer in person and began to make my way to the door, I caught him out of the corner of my eye doing a "happy dance" down the hallway. By referring her to us, he'd saved one of his best clients $60,000 a year, and had become Janet's hero. I have never met Janet personally and probably never will, but if you can get a trust officer to do a "happy dance," you know you have done something right!

How did I know what to do for Janet? And when clients ask, "What is *the best policy*, anyway?" what do you tell them?

What all grantors need to know: **the best policy is the one that's right for *you*.**

"Well, how do I know which policy is right for me?" a client might ask. Have your clients take into consideration the following: *What are your needs today? If you have an existing policy already in force, how have your needs changed since you first purchased the policy?* Remember to ask why—and in asking why, you'll have taken the first step toward making your ILIT into something you really <u>can</u> trust, in the most basic sense of the word. At my firm, LifeTrust3D, LLC, we utilize a comprehensive questionnaire that asks these essential questions and more, and this questionnaire helps us ascertain a client's true needs.

With Janet, we assessed her current needs, considered the best policy for her, and then re-engineered the structure so that she truly could have *the best policy*. In its simplest form, "re-engineering" a policy through a policy exchange is similar to refinancing a home. Home mortgages used to charge 7 or 8 percent interest, and even 20 percent in the 80s, but today, in 2015, mortgages tend to be between 3 and 5 percent. As a result, it's to a homeowner's benefit to refinance if they haven't already done so. Most eligible homeowners who qualify have already re-financed their mortgages. Today, life insurance policy exchanges are becoming less of an option because many "eligible" candidates have already refinanced their insurance programs.

Life changes, and so does the economy. There are several options for re-engineering existing policies, such as changing a dividend option within the existing policy, reducing a term rider, increasing the premiums, or even selecting a "reduced, paid-up" policy from the insurance carrier. Although both Charles and Janet benefitted from a policy exchange, in most cases re-engineering the current policy most likely produces the *best policy* for a client if their needs have changed. Everyone's needs are different, so each case is unique, but the goal is always the same: to have policies that fit clients' needs

> Life changes, and so does the economy. There are several options for re-engineering existing policies, such as changing a dividend option within the policy, reducing a term rider, increasing the premiums, or even selecting a "reduced, paid-up" policy from the insurance carrier.

today. In fact, our firm's research into hundreds of policy reviews indicates that the frequency with which replacements make sense is decreasing by the year.

> It's important to be able to ask the client, "Are your needs still the same as when you first put this policy in place?" If not, the follow-up needs to be, "How have those needs changed, and how can we adapt to make your policy reasonable for your current circumstances?"

Purposeful, comprehensive insurance design isn't just an analytical review of the policy or a comparison to a different policy. A complete life insurance review involves all parties: the estate planning attorney, the investment advisor, the grantor, the trustee, and most important, the family members. It's important to be able to ask the client, "Are your needs still the same as when you first put this policy in place?" If not, the follow-up needs to be, "How have those needs changed, and how can we adapt to make your policy reasonable for your current circumstances?" Sometimes a policy needs to be re-engineered because the client purchased it when the estate tax exemption was lower. Maybe the client has adult children who might benefit more from immediate financial support than they would from a large, lump-sum inheritance at the time of the insured's death. Or perhaps the client's ability to fund the premiums has changed. The possibilities are endless, and it's necessary to consider as many as possible.

When working with numbers, it's easy to forget the personal element behind all this. These are people's lives. They bought life insurance primarily because they wanted to provide for their loved ones, not solely because they care about a sophisticated estate plan. In effectively assessing a trust-owned life insurance policy, there are five fundamental factors to examine.

Premium

The first question to ask is, **"Has your ability or desire to fund premiums changed?"** You may find that the $60,000 premium a client was able to fund in 1988 is no longer reasonable with his or her current income (as was the case with Janet). Or you might find that the client's income and the estate's value have skyrocketed since the initial purchase of the policy, and there's now a need to increase the client's assets outside of their taxable estate. A premium may also need to be increased or decreased depending on the client's health, life expectancy, and/or family history.

Death Benefit

The next question is, **"Does the death benefit still apply to your situation?"** Maybe a grantor's estate has grown substantially and he or she is able to leave more behind. Maybe a client *needs* to leave more assets than he or she previously anticipated. Maybe the client has children who became wealthier than expected and don't need the money. Or maybe the client has grown estranged from his or her family and wants the money to be redirected to a favorite charity instead. When one of my client's relationships with his children had soured, he decided to leave his inheritance to a local hospital. His situation had simply changed, so we needed to reassess. This is when collaboration with an estate planning attorney becomes invaluable.

Health

"How's your health presently?" is the third question on the list. If someone's having health difficulties, it may make sense to adjust the premiums. For example, if an eighty-year-old is suffering from a life-threatening illness and has a $1 million life insurance policy that is designed to stay in force until age one hundred, he or she may not need to continue funding the current $20,000 annual premium. With careful planning and collaboration, the premiums could potentially be eliminated or reduced and the policy kept in force until age eighty-five or ninety so that more money is not paid into the contract than necessary (depending on the policy type and its structure). It's all a question of the individual's situation, which can be monitored by continually asking, "Why?"

Performance

The fourth question is, **"How long is the policy projected to stay in force based on reasonable earning assumptions and current premium funding?"** In the sustained, low interest-rate environment that the United States is experiencing, we're finding that more and more policies initially thought to be ones that would stay in force throughout a client's lifetime will lapse before the client passes away. Insurance companies aren't able to credit the dividend that they were able to when returns on fixed income portfolios were higher, and the result is that policies may not be meeting their original expectations.

Risk

> The key is to find the *best* combination of cost-effective premiums, the *best* financially stable carrier, the *best* secondary death benefit guarantee, the *best* potential for future flexibility, and most importantly, the *best* ongoing commitment for policy management and monitoring.

Our last crucial question is, **"How much risk are you willing to take on?"** There's risk and rewards, advantages and disadvantages in every type of policy, and it's crucial that the extent of these factors reflect a client's risk tolerance. There's risk in having all of a client's cash value rely solely on general account products (such as Universal or Whole Life policies), or on the performance of the investment sub-accounts within a separate account, a variable policy. It's important for clients to understand the rewards and risks of having said policy. They might have a policy with strong contractual guarantees and low premiums, but chances are that they'll be giving up future flexibility gained through cash value accumulation in exchange for those low premiums. The question then becomes—do they understand what this might mean for them in the future, and are they okay with those repercussions?

There's risk and reward in every type of insurance policy. The *best policy* matches a client's tolerance for risk with the rewards a client wants to reap. The key is to find the *best* combination of cost-effective premiums, the *best* financially stable carrier, the *best* secondary death benefit guarantee (for ILITs, I generally recommend guarantees to at least life expectancy), the *best* potential for future flexibility, and most importantly, the *best* ongoing commitment for policy management and monitoring. Remember, ILITs are dynamic, not

Carriers have a way of finding out about the risks they take on when insuring policyholders through databases such as the Medical Information Bureau, motor vehicle reports, prescription searches, and IRS records. To avoid surprises, our firm utilizes a Private Underwriting Rating Evaluation Process for our clients, which allows us to assess all aspects of the client's insurability before making any decisions.

static ... and the only thing that is certain in life is change!

Underwriting

For individuals seeking new life insurance, the element that has the most impact on insurance carrier selection and product pricing is the underwriting process. Many consumers believe that you purchase life insurance with premium dollars, but it's more complicated than that. You purchase it first with your health, good character, and financial stability, and *then* with your premium dollars. Carriers have a way of finding out about the risks they take on when insuring policyholders through databases such as the Medical Information Bureau, motor vehicle reports, prescription searches, and IRS records. To avoid surprises, our firm utilizes a Private Underwriting Rating Evaluation (PURE) Process for our clients. The process allows us to assess all aspects of the client's insurability prior to finalizing any insurance recommendation or completing a formal life insurance application. If there are any potential issues with prospective life insurance consumers, we want to find out up front and then navigate the insurance landscape appropriately, using the decades of life insurance expertise we have acquired.

•••

At the beginning of 2011, as he approached age sixty-five, my client Guy began to see a need to provide more for his family during his lifetime. Guy and his wife, Claire, had three adult daughters whom they loved dearly. Two of their daughters had special needs children, and the third was struggling to start a small business—and they all needed their parents' help. Guy and Claire were already grantors of an irrevocable life trust, but it was a second-to-die policy, meaning that their daughters wouldn't receive any benefits until both parents had passed away. The policy had been created when Guy's daughters were young and he and Claire traveled extensively. His daughters were now grown, but they still needed their dad.

The insurance company was not as financially stable as it once had been, and Guy began to worry that the company wouldn't be able to make good on the promise it had originally made to him and his family and pay the correct benefit when the time came. At the time, the cash value of the policy was $950,000. The policy itself, which had a death benefit of $5 million, was relatively outdated, and needed a lot of cash in order to perform the way Guy had hoped it would. His other assets weren't liquid, as he was invested heavily in commercial real estate. The question became, how could he adequately fund his policy and yet still support his family?

In re-engineering his policy, Guy wanted to keep most of his numbers the same. He had been making an annual gift to the trust of $15,000, which worked quite well for him. He also wanted the trust to maintain a $5 million life insurance value for the benefit of his daughters. We faced two hurdles with Guy and Claire:

Guy and Claire wanted to engineer a lifetime distribution from the trust to their daughters. Ensuring this kind of payout is not an easy task, and we had to work hard with the trust beneficiaries and the corporate ILIT trustee to approve the distribution. After submitting proof to the trustee that his daughters needed financial assistance to support their families, we were able to receive distribution during Guy's lifetime—a rare occurrence. The trustee's duty is to provide the maximum possible benefit for the trust beneficiaries, and it gets more and more difficult to achieve that goal if money is taken out of the trust during the grantor's lifetime. This type of distribution can only occur if the proper "HEMS" language is contained within the trust document (HEMS stands for "Health, Education, Maintenance, and Support"). Guy's daughters needed all of the above, making it possible for distribution to occur.

With survivorship (second-to-die) life insurance, the majority of the pricing is dictated by the wife's health and age (because we all know women live longer than men!). Claire, however, hated medical examinations involving blood work and needles, and such examinations are the procedures most commonly used by insurance companies to determine pricing. Fortunately, we were able to learn through our PURE process that Claire had had regular physician check-ups, and all indications showed that she was in excellent health. We found one carrier that would make an exception and allow us to forego blood work and issue a Standard, Non-Smoker underwriting classification to her. After reviewing the medical records, the insurance carrier knew Claire would have qualified for Preferred Best underwriting, but for Claire, an improved rate class just wasn't worth the "pain" of the blood work required.

> The trustee's duty is to provide the maximum possible benefit for the trust beneficiaries, and it gets more and more difficult to achieve that goal if money is taken out of the trust during the grantor's lifetime.

Working closely with the trustee, we were able to exchange policies and keep all of Guy's numbers the same (a $5 million death benefit and a $15,000 premium), help the family find a more efficient policy to fit their needs, *and* receive some distribution from the $950,000 cash value—which was everything Guy had hoped for. *The best policy* for Guy, it turned out, was one with a stronger carrier that could withstand the test of time and allow him the flexibility necessary to help his family.

On Christmas Eve of 2011, Guy and I were able to deposit $100,000 into each of his daughters' bank accounts. On December 26, I received a personal phone call from each of his daughters, thanking me. By taking the time to re-engineer his policy entirely, Guy and I had made a world of difference to his children—and that's our goal, as it always should be.

As trustees and advisors consider how to make each policy more purposeful, don't forget to ask: why? Why was this policy purchased and why is it needed today? The answers to these questions will put you on the path to creating *the best policy*.

5

Who's in the Cockpit, Anyway? Why a Prudent Process Matters Now More than Ever

IF YOU'VE EVER traveled far, you're probably familiar with the grueling routine of getting on an airplane. You drag yourself through check-in and airport security to the gate, wait for another forty-five minutes, and finally are allowed to board the plane. As the plane takes off, you fall asleep, sure that the hardest part of your travel is over now that the plane is in the air.

Can you imagine waking up mid-flight to find that there's actually no one in the cockpit, and you have no way to take control of the plane? Sure, that scenario is a bit outlandish, but it's exactly what the owners and beneficiaries of many life insurance policies are facing today. Arriving at your destination safely requires prudent planning. If we think of an ILIT in the estate-planning context, as a vehicle to accomplish plans for the client, it can be likened to a long aircraft flight that transfers estate assets to a specified destination—the intended beneficiaries. There are numerous parties involved in the pre-flight planning, yet the ultimate success of the flight relies on the expertise of the pilot flying the plane. Unfortunately, there is a disturbing trend that threatens to undermine the best laid plans: the absence of any pilot once the journey has begun. The abandonment of life insurance policies by the parties who are supposed to be managing them and ensuring that they stay on course over time will undoubtedly cause irreparable harm to the policies' performance, and eventually to the beneficiaries.

A Different Kind of Asset

In the management of a client's investment assets, active monitoring and reporting is now the standard. Assets should be reviewed periodically, and rebalanced and adjusted based on performance, economic considerations, and the client's goals and objectives. The consequences of an underperforming investment portfolio aren't typically dire, and there are myriad ways to take corrective action. With a life insurance policy, though, underperformance can terminate assets, and options for corrective action are limited once the damage has been done.

Life insurance policies purchased for the purpose of providing long-term death benefits often span multiple decades. Few other assets owned as widely as life insurance have such a lengthy duration, or such a material financial impact on beneficiaries. Compared to other financial instruments, life insurance is much less liquid due to various barriers (financial, health-related, or tax-related) to entry and exit. Thus, life insurance requires an uncommon combination of due diligence up front, and ongoing monitoring within a sometimes confining set of boundaries.

Flying Through a Turbulence Zone

When it comes to pre-purchase product research, the knowledge of the consumer has increased tremendously in the last decade. Much has been written about the selection and structure of life insurance policies, and in the age of the Internet, most of this material is very accessible. Professional continuing education sessions on life insurance are widely available as well. As such, it is likely that at least one of a client's professional advisors (attorney, trustee, financial advisor, or accountant) has *some* exposure to the life insurance acquisition process, and they'll typically assist in the purchasing process to some degree. Unfortunately, this tends to be where the practical assistance ends, and the policy owner is often left alone with a strange and complicated asset.

> The problem is that risks are most prevalent *after* policy purchase. Prior to purchase, great care is taken to ensure a proper balance within ownership, but potential threats such as premium timing, change in beneficiaries, loan strategies, and more are all risks to the policy's ultimate success.

The problem with this approach is that risks are most prevalent *after* policy purchase. Prior to purchase, great care is taken to ensure a proper balance within ownership, but potential threats such as premium timing, change in beneficiaries, loan strategies, and more are all risks to the policy's ultimate success. Unintended but possible changes, like premium suspension, death benefit reductions, or dividend options also typically have to be considered, as do various tax implications.

What happens if a plane is lacking expert guidance as it flies through a storm system? It may not get to the destination; the passengers may get hurt; and at the very least, it's going to be a turbulent, unpleasant flight. What, then, are the consequences if these risks to a policy manifest and aren't properly addressed over time?

The consequences may be financial in nature, and they may be less obvious to the naked eye. The most obvious repercussions are increased out-of-pocket premium requirements, reductions in the death benefit, lower cash value, or loss of coverage prior to death. When these things go awry, there may be side effects too—for example, gift or income taxes may be incurred. In cases in which coverage is reduced or terminated and the life insurance was a key foundation in a planning strategy, there could be a wide range of consequences, such as the inability to properly transfer business interests, unequal estate distributions to heirs, lack of liquidity, or forced sales of assets that were never intended to be sold.

Just as a plane is affected by internal and external forces, so is a life insurance policy. The grantor of an irrevocable life insurance trust can't manage the policy. The insurance agent or broker, attorney, and accountant may have no legal or contractual duty after the policy's been sold, which should scare grantors and beneficiaries—a *lot*. So who, then, is sitting in the cockpit managing the policy and reacting to the external forces?

The burden rests solely in the hands of the trustee. The trustee, whether professional or non-, has to guide the policy through all kinds of storms to a destination that is thirty, forty, or even fifty years in the future. The Uniform Prudent Investors Act (UPIA) provides a fairly detailed set of standards to describe what the trustee should be doing, as well as specific practices to measure whether they are exercising adequate care of the assets. Bank trustees may be more cognizant of management principles through 2012 Office of the Comptroller of the Currency (OCC) guidelines.

Given the well-established fiduciary standard of a trustee, one would think that a policy would always be treated professionally and with great care. However, a disturbing trend has emerged in recent years that should concern grantors and beneficiaries alike. There's been a movement that effectively provides a parachute for some trustees to escape the plane. This trend, either by statute or trust provision, may absolve the trustee of his or her responsibilities to the beneficiaries regarding the outcome of the policy (excluding, of course, any outright fraud or criminal acts). As of 2012, at least thirteen states have enacted statutes that do not hold a trustee responsible for any losses sustained to a policy. Similar statutes have been or are currently being proposed in other states, and such protections by statute or provision may be afforded to trust advisors as well.

While this kind of statute or provision might be a reasonable request coming from a family member or friend acting as trustee, the inclusion of such language for professional trustees seems unreasonable. Clients entrust their assets to professionals and pay them for professional trustee services, and the hope is that these professionals will then take care of the client to the best of their ability. A February 2014 article in *Trusts & Estates* magazine poses an interesting question to attorneys: "How many of our settlors would proceed with their trusts if they really understood that their beneficiaries had no enforceable rights in the event of gross negligence or even reckless misconduct of the trustee, or of any misconduct, incompetence, or negligence of the non-fiduciary advisor, short of outright fraud?"[1]

Even without these "parachutes," two court cases in particular seem to set a very low standard for the duties the trustee must satisfy to avoid liability for the outcome of his or her actions. In *Cochran v. Keybank*[2], it was deemed that, in regards to the replacement of an existing policy by a new policy with a 65 percent lower death benefit and $107,764 in surrender charges, it was sufficient that the trustee "examined the viability of existing policies and at least one other option." In *French v. Wachovia Bank*[3], the trust documents gave the trustee the discretion to "retain, invest, and reinvest in any property ... regardless of any risk, lack of diversification, or unproductivity involved ... to continue as trustee and to deal with any trust hereunder without regards to conflicts of interest." This language allowed the trustee to engage in self-dealing by purchasing new life insurance from the bank's insurance brokerage affiliate.

---

1 Bove Jr., Alexander A., *The Death of the Trust*, Trusts & Estates, p. 51-55, Feb. 2014
2 In re Stuart Cochran Irrevocable Trust, 901 N.E.2d 1128 (Indiana Court of Appeals, March 2, 2009)
3 French v. Wachovia Bank, N.A., 2011 U.S. Dist. LEXIS 72808 (E.D. Wisconsin 2011)

Cochran v. KeyBank

- 1987: Cochran purchases $4.75MM Universal Life and Whole Life insurance portfolio
- 1999: stock market races; Cochran's insurance agent replaces existing policies with Variable Universal Life and increases death benefit to $8MM
- 2001: Stock market declines, nationwide panic ensues
- 2003: $8MM was exchanged for a $2.5MM Guaranteed Universal Life Policy
- 2004: Cochran dies

French v. Wachovia Bank

- 2003: French owns two Whole Life policies with $5MM death benefit and $2.2MM cash value
- 2004: Whole Life policies and cash value exchanged for $5MM Guaranteed Universal Life with $0 premiums, saving trust $620K. However, cash value decreases due to new policy type and sizeable commission
- French's reaction: claims "self-dealing" and that Wachovia, by earning over $500K in commissions, failed its duty of loyalty by putting its own interest before that of the beneficiaries

These were two early court cases that have favorably impacted the way life insurance policies are generally managed, especially if including a bank trustee. I've witnessed banks—national and community alike—taking prudent policy management much more seriously by strengthening their internal support systems. Banks have also started to take advantage of third-party review firms, which is recommended in section nine of the Uniform Prudent Investor Act.

•••

Consider the following possible scenarios in which a trustee could conceivably be viewed as negligent if his or her actions adversely affected the policy:

- A trustee pays the premium late or early, either of which might result in a higher required premium or loss of policy guarantees.
- A trustee fails to change investment allocations and leaves money in the money market account, even though the policy requires an earnings rate approaching 8 percent in order to sustain itself.
- A trustee initiates a policy distribution prior to maturity of an earnings segment, causing forfeiture of five years of index policy gains.
- A trustee deactivates the dollar cost averaging feature, which results in permanent termination of the policy's guaranteed death benefit provisions.

- A trustee isn't aware of a looming policy lapse because of failure to secure periodic re-projections of policy performance.
- A trustee fails to recognize upcoming deadlines in the policy death benefit and/or significant premium increases because of reliance upon abbreviated policy information provided by the carrier.

Given these possible pitfalls and the adverse effect of that any one of these scenarios might have—combined with the possibility that no one is in the pilot seat in the first place— gone are the days of assuming a trust-owned life insurance contract can go unmanaged. Grantors, be certain to read and understand trust language in your document, or simply be sure to ask your trustee if they are taking proactive steps in managing and monitoring your policy. If not, you should look to a proactive life insurance advisor whom you do have confidence in. You might also prefer to seek out a trustee who has a prudent policy management system. Yes, it might come at a slightly higher fee—but trust me, you want someone you can *trust* flying your plane and navigating around any dangers that lie ahead.

ILITs with a non-professional trustee scare me the most. Why? Oftentimes, Crummey notices aren't

Grantors, be certain to read and understand trust language in your document, or simply be sure to ask your trustee if they are taking proactive steps in managing and monitoring your policy. If not, you should look to a proactive life insurance advisor whom you do have confidence in. You might also prefer to seek out a trustee who has a prudent policy management system.

executed and stored properly (or at all), or an annual statement is mistaken for a policy review and policy performance is left to happenstance. Don't get me wrong—I have seen some ILITs with non-professional trustees work quite well, but only for the most astute, detailed-oriented, and organized parties. Understandably, grantors may not want to pay what they feel are too expensive fees for a professional trustee, or they may not want to answer to a corporate trustee. All too frequently, though, we have witnessed scenarios where if a professional advisor isn't involved on an annual basis or if an attorney hasn't trained the trustee properly in relation to their duties to ensure trustee administration duties are carried out correctly, paying or not paying fees simply won't matter in the long run. If ILITs are not administered properly, the IRS may find upon audit that if the ILIT hasn't met specified guidelines, life insurance proceeds may be subject to estate taxes. If you are unsure whether your ILIT is being administered properly, be sure to refresh yourself with the flow chart on page 20 and contact your estate planning attorney.

Does any of this mean that every trustee will abandon their duties? Certainly not. Most trustees do take their fiduciary responsibilities very seriously, and as noted, some banks have taken a leadership role in modeling a prudent process, even employing third-party, fee-based reviews of life insurance policies. In any case, making sure a pilot is in the pilot's seat gives all parties to the trust the best chance of a successful flight.

Securing a Pilot and a Flight Plan

As noted, we simply can't make the assumption that someone is looking out for what might happen to an ILIT down the road, or taking the necessary steps to give the policy the best possible chance of achieving the desired outcome. What, then, can we do to make sure the policy is being regularly monitored and managed over time?

STEP 1: *Creating a Flight Plan*

For an ILIT, a flight plan takes the form of a life insurance policy management statement. It is necessary to understand the environment and constraints under which policy-related decisions should be made. Why was the policy established? Are there targeted policy earnings levels required to sustain said policy? Is there a reason for a concentrated carrier position, rather than a portfolio of policies from multiple carriers? Are there limits on grantor contributions for premium payments? Are there any events or developments that should trigger specific actions, including consideration of alternative policies? Has the need for the policy changed, or the grantor's desire to fund premium gifts changed (a common situation with today's higher estate tax exemption amounts)?

A tangible, written-out policy management statement can document these considerations, as well as many others that can then be used to manage the ILIT. Consider incorporation of trust language that is related to the use of the policy management statement (including provisions for periodic revision of standards as necessary). With such a document, all involved parties will be better informed and held accountable from the beginning. The written policy management statement also lays a foundation upon which to judge any proposed new or replacement policies.

STEP 2: *Ongoing Policy Management and Monitoring*

While it's impractical for every individual trust to have a specialized policy service system or process, it's *not* impractical for a grantor to insist that any policies be managed by a party employing such a system. A robust policy management process or software system can provide functionality such as basic policy reporting, premium reminders, status checks, measurement against standards established in the management statement, carrier financial reporting, and even document storage capabilities. While this step may require a fee to be incurred, there are too many things that can go wrong in the future with policies that rely solely on ad-hoc reporting. For new coverage being purchased, consider only agents who employ (and can demonstrate consistently) a system or process with such capabilities. Consider incorporating language into the trust document that

A robust policy management process or software system can provide functionality such as basic policy reporting, premium reminders, status checks, measurement against standards established in the management statement, carrier financial reporting, and even document storage capabilities. requires the trustee to employ such a system, whether internally or via outsourcing to a qualified third party. (It would also be prudent to employ such a system for policies that are not trust-owned.)

STEP 3: *Written Contract with a Competent Flight Crew*

Discuss the obligations and responsibilities of the trustee with your legal counsel. If you're uncomfortable with the language, look for a trustee willing to provide appropriate services without shirking fiduciary responsibilities. It may require greater administrative fees or a change in trust situs, but those may be reasonable accommodations for the peace of mind that comes with an experienced pilot flying your plane.

It is insufficient to rely on annual statements as a life insurance management tool. Policy statements are just snapshots of a point in time, and they usually don't accurately re-project the expected performance of the policy in the future. Include language in your management statement requiring periodic (annual, bi-annual, or tri-annual) in-force illustrations to be obtained. However, make sure that the data can be properly interpreted and acted upon. If you haven't been trained to read an EKG correctly, then merely having a printed EKG does little to help you make a diagnosis. You need someone capable of interpreting the results, identifying any potential problems, and developing any necessary plan of action.

Reporting is most useful in conjunction with consultation. Make sure that that consultation is with a qualified third party who can provide interpretation and advice related to the information as necessary, and who has the ability to act efficiently on any required modifications. What if there needs to be an explanation or discussion with trust beneficiaries or grantors? Who is willing and capable of such a task? Many third-party reporting solutions fail to provide the crucial element of interpretation and consultation, stopping only at report generation.

It is equally important that any policy management services also include some level of "fulfillment" services. Analyzing, planning, and adapting are important to the long-term success of a life insurance plan, but any changes have to be implemented properly. Is the agent still around? Is the agent willing to assist? (Remember, the agent may not have a contractual obligation to service the policy—although the good ones do take this seriously.) What if modifications require careful timing and coordination due to legal, tax, or accounting considerations? Who's managing the implementation? Consideration should be given to the ability of policy managers to coordinate and manage the implementation of any requisite modifications. "Reporting only" service providers may leave trustees flying solo when it comes to making changes.

Ideally, an agent is willing to commit—in writing—to providing a given level of policy service, and can provide the policy management system, necessary reporting, interpretation, consultation, and implementation. A simple policy service contract can outline the services the agent is willing to provide for the policy. There may be an annual fee associated with the management activities, but it's money well spent in order to give the ILIT the best possibility of producing your desired outcome.

> Section 9 of the UPIA specifically addresses Delegation of Investment and Management Functions. Under Section 9, the trustee may reduce risk while providing a best-practices approach to the management and monitoring of ILIT policies.

In absence of a written policy management contract with the writing agent, many trust companies and other professional trustees are now delegating some duties to third-party, fee-based policy management and monitoring firms. Generally, this has resulted in the trustees increasing their fees. Section 9 of the UPIA specifically addresses Delegation of Investment and Management Functions. Under Section 9, the trustee may reduce risk while providing a best-practices approach to the management and monitoring of ILIT policies.

Table 1 – Differences in managing investment portfolios and life insurance

Trust Investment Portfolio	ILIT Life Insurance Policy
Under-performance results in lower portfolio balances.	Under-performance may result in loss of the entire policy and may have tax implications
Near limitless investment options and strategies to recover from portfolio underperformance including: change allocations, find lower fees, change managers, change durations, add more money, or increase risk exposure.	Investment choices (if any) and options to recover are dictated by the type of policy, policy funding limits, and other factors. It may not be possible to change allocations, lower fees, add money, change durations or alter the risk exposure.
Easy to quantify cost to put an investment strategy back on track.	May be difficult or even impossible to quantify the ultimate cost to put a life insurance strategy back on track.
An investment portfolio might have lower expense levels over time as the asset base grows.	Many policies have significantly escalating expenses over time.
It is simple to change the risk profile or time horizon of an investment portfolio.	A policy may not allow a change in the investment risk profile or the investment time horizon.
Borrowing or distributions from an investment portfolio can be easily quantified and modeled under a variety of assumptions and fact patterns.	The full impact of a loan, partial surrender or distribution from a life insurance policy may not be easily determined prior to execution or even disclosed in some policy types.
Relatively easy to diversify a portfolio at any time without inordinate increases in associated expenses.	Available underwriting offers and product types may result in significantly higher costs for carrier diversification and is available up front only.
The trustee may unilaterally choose to liquidate one or more investment positions.	While a trustee may surrender a policy outright, he may not execute a life settlement without consent of the insured.
There is significant breadth and depth of research and insight on investment strategies and portfolios.	Sound research and insight on life insurance policies is difficult to find. What information is out there is often plagued by omission or supposition of fact patterns or actions.
Many trustees are very knowledgeable on investments and investment strategies.	Few trustees are experts on life insurance.
Some investments may have barriers to exit such as income taxes, capital gains taxes, back end loads, surrender charge periods, notice requirements, or lock up periods.	A life insurance policy has barriers to exit that may include income taxes, surrender charges, forfeiture of earnings, notice requirements, lock up periods, and delays for receipt of surrender proceeds.
Some investments may have barriers to entry such as minimum investment requirements.	Life insurance policies have significant barriers to entry including willingness and consent of the insured party to undergo underwriting, health worthiness of the insured, a pricing structure that escalates with age, and restrictions on minimum and maximum allowable premiums.

Recognition that the traditional life insurance management process is inherently flawed, as well as modification of behavior, will help you to avoid any challenges during flight. The steps suggested in this chapter can provide additional assurance to grantors, beneficiaries, and trustees that the flight has the best chance of reaching the intended destination—while minimizing turbulence as much as possible.

6

How Can Fiduciaries Effectively Monitor and Manage Policies?

AT LIFETRUST3D, LLC, our 3D Process™, means continual management, monitoring, and review of your ever-changing policies—each of which will take into account the complex factors in this life. Our process is built to assist fiduciaries in meeting the standards set forth by both the Uniform Prudent Investor Act (UPIA) and the Office of the Comptroller of the Currency (OCC).

The UPIA

Established to focus on the entire portfolio's performance, the UPIA requires that a trustee acting in his or her fiduciary capacity demonstrate a particular process for selecting, managing, and monitoring all assets held in the trust. Fortunately, the UPIA is focused on process (as opposed to outcome), which means that fiduciaries are held to a certain standard as they assist their clients.

As of May 2004, forty-four states as well as Washington, D.C. have adopted the act.

The UPIA has five major governing principles:

1. The standard of prudence is applied to any investment as part of the total portfolio, rather than individual investments ... "portfolio" embraces all assets.
2. The tradeoff in all investing between risk and return is identified as the fiduciary's central consideration.
3. All categoric restrictions on types of investments have been abrogated; the trustee can invest in anything that plays an appropriate role in achieving the risk/return objectives of the trust and that meets the other requirements of prudent investing.
4. The long familiar requirement that fiduciaries diversify their investments has been integrated into the definition of prudent investing.
5. The much-criticized former rule of trust law forbidding the trustee to delegate investment and management functions has been reversed.[4]

---

4 Section 9, *Uniform Prudent Investment Act*, 1995

The UPIA is determined by the National Conference of Commissioners on Uniform State Laws, but most importantly, it sets a precedent for how fiduciaries should engage in their work. Prior to the passage of this act, there was no standard ethical code that held fiduciaries accountable for their decisions. In the UPIA, fiduciaries find a code of conduct for advisory and management—a guide that not only encourages, but legally requires cultivating a best policy for each client. We take those same ideas that have long been accepted in the investment world and help make them more accessible to fiduciaries in our world of life insurance. We want everyone to give every policy its due diligence.

There are nine sections of the UPIA, each of which provides detail to help trustees and fiduciaries uphold those five principles.

SECTION 1: *The Prudent Investor Rule*
First and foremost, the UPIA declares that a trustee who invests and manages assets owes a duty to the beneficiaries. In other words, trustees: treat others as you'd want to be treated. Section 1 is the Golden Rule that carries the rest of the Act, and it's the code that all advisors should live by, whether they are involved with life insurance or other facets of the industry.

SECTION 2: *Standard of Care; Portfolio Strategy; Risk and Return Objectives*
Section 2 requires a trustee to deeply consider each investment, paying attention to the various risks and the *purpose* of each policy, and how it all affects the portfolio as a whole.

SECTION 3: *Diversification*
This section advises trustees and advisors to diversify portfolios (unless the portfolio is better served by not diversifying).

SECTION 4: *Duties at Inception of Trusteeship*
Section 4 requires a trustee to consider each asset's contribution to the portfolio and dispose of unsuitable assets within a reasonable time period if necessary.

SECTION 5: *Loyalty*
Beneficiaries need to feel as though someone's on their side; section 5 of the UPIA encourages trustees and advisors to remain loyal to the beneficiaries and act in their best interest.

SECTION 6: *Impartiality*
This section takes care of those trusts that have

more than one beneficiary; the trustee must make fair decisions that are in the interest of *all* the beneficiaries. This concept is derived from Section 5 (loyalty).

SECTION 7: *Investment Costs*
Section 7 requires trustees to mitigate costs, only incurring those that are reasonable and in the best interest of the portfolio and the beneficiaries.

SECTION 8: *Reviewing Compliance*
Section 8 addresses our question of "how does your policy meet your needs today?" In other words, compliance with the UPIA is determined by the current factors, rather than those in the past.

SECTION 9: *Delegation of Investment and Management*
Crucial to ILIT trustees is Section 9 of the UPIA, which allows delegation and actually provides fiduciaries with safeguards. Working with a third party is now not just accepted—it's the common practice among all the large national banks, and regional and community banks with trust departments are now following suit. Trustees

can now figure out which parts of the insurance policy review they can reasonably, comfortably, and productively complete in-house, and they can delegate those aspects that are not necessarily within their skill set to a third party.

Strengths of the UPIA

The UPIA protects and supports trustees who have a prudent and disciplined process (sections 1, 2, 4). Understand that some states do have an exculpatory statute under which trustees can specify that they are not liable if a policy fails—but regardless of these statutes, the act (and our process) is designed to help provide maximum benefits to the beneficiaries while reducing risk to the trustees. In states where these statutes do exist, support for grantors is not necessarily strong, because trustees aren't held accountable. In cases like these it's particularly helpful to have a trusted advisor on hand to make sure that those policies are being handled accordingly. National banks are leading the way in instituting a due diligence process that follows the UPIA closely.

There's no eliminating risk, but there are efficacious technology platforms and third-party firms available that can help streamline the policy management process, saving trustees time, energy, and effort (UPIA section 9). With these platforms, administration can define the policy management criteria, such as desired death benefit, policy lapse age, carrier financial strength, and recommended premium funding. With their advisor, clients can define agreed-upon measurement criteria (a flight plan). So if, for example, a trustee specifies that a policy is to stay in force until at least age 100, and the projection shows that it will only stay in force until age eighty-five, the trustee will know right away that he or she has to increase the premium, decrease the death benefit, or find another viable alternative.

The UPIA also requires trustees to make reasonable and sound judgments about the return rates of

There's no eliminating risk, but there are efficacious technology platforms and third-party firms available that can help streamline the policy management process, saving trustees time, energy, and effort. With these platforms, administration can define the policy management criteria, such as desired death benefit, policy lapse age, and recommended premium funding.

policies. A strong company is a great start, but with a weak plan design, a portfolio may not achieve all that it was intended to achieve.

We recently reviewed a contract for Kathryn, a sixty-eight-year-old woman in excellent health. Kathryn had a $2 million policy with one of the strongest insurance companies in the marketplace, and she was funding the policy with $15,000 annual premiums. Even with a strong carrier, Kathryn's policy was going to lapse once she reached age eighty-six. According to the 2008 VBO Mortality Tables, the life expectancy of a healthy sixty-eight-year-old woman is eighty-nine. (The definition of life expectancy is the projected age at which less than half of that population will still be alive.)

The interest rate on Kathryn's policy was 4 percent, but in order to keep the policy from lapsing, it would be necessary to re-engineer; the policy was sold in the 90s, when the assumed interest crediting rate on the original illustration was 7 percent. There were options: we could increase the premium to $22,000 to keep the policy projecting to stay in force to age one hundred, or we could change the death benefit from $2 million to $1.4 million and still have a viable policy that would be there for Kathryn's whole life.

Making a decision like this one requires a certain amount of thought, and it's thought that may not have been given when Kathryn initially purchased the policy. What likely happened was that the trust officer saw the strong carrier and a reassuring sales illustration and didn't feel the need to dig deeper. In outsourcing these kinds of decisions to a third party, a trust officer who may not know any better can put their clients' policies in the hands of an expert who can and will carefully analyze each aspect of the policy and take *all* aspects into account—not just the excellent reputation of the insurance company.

The UPIA also advises fiduciaries to diversify within each portfolio where possible, as any financial advisor would do with an investment portfolio. The old adage is never more true than in the context of managing an ILIT; remember, these are people's lives and livelihoods that we're managing, and we want to be cautious and deliberate with our choices. The UPIA is an excellent guide for managing policies because it provides a framework for fiduciaries and encourages them to take a close look and monitor *actively*.

The OCC

The OCC has standards similar to those of the UPIA and is another guide to serving and protecting all parties involved in a life insurance policy, emphasizing the responsibility bank fiduciaries have toward their clients.

The language specifies that the fiduciary should fully understand each policy and explore its options, and also encourages the employment of a third party if the fiduciary is unable to do so. Most critically, it outlines the criteria that a fiduciary should consider in the maintenance of policies:

> *The OCC ... continues to require bank fiduciaries ... to conduct annual investment reviews of all assets of each fiduciary account for which the bank has investment discretion. This review should evaluate the financial health of the issuing insurance company as well as whether the policy is performing as illustrated or whether replacement should be considered ... Independent of these reviews, a fiduciary bank must have risk management systems and reviews that address the following:*
>
> - **Sufficiency of premiums:** *The bank fiduciary must determine whether current premiums are sufficient to maintain the policy to maturity or to meet the insured's life expectancy.*
> - **Suitability of the insurance policy:** *Consider replacing an insurance policy if the bank fiduciary identifies concerns with the*

condition of the insurance provider or if that provider does not meet the needs of the grantor or beneficiaries. Also assess any tax changes that could affect the suitability of the policy.

- **Carrier selection:** *The bank fiduciary needs to evaluate the carrier's financial condition. To the extent insurance carrier ratings are available, they generally lag corporate and market events, and should be used principally as indicators of a firm's creditworthiness.*

- **Appropriateness of investment strategy:** *The bank fiduciary must evaluate the appropriateness of investments of any segregated account of support the cash value.*[5]

The following tips are some of the more important ones to help trustees stay on track:

1. A policy management statement and/or guidelines for each ILIT, or a flight plan (as described in chapter three). A policy

---

5 Office of the Comptroller of the Currency, Administrator of National Banks, *Comptroller's Handbook*, 2002, p. 37-39

management statement establishes, clarifies, and solidifies the monitoring criteria you'll follow for that particular trust, just as you might do for an investment portfolio. In a policy management statement, you'll determine the parameters for policy lapse age, premium funding, insurance carrier financial strength, crediting rate, and death benefit—all the details that need to be taken into account in order to create and maintain *the best policy* for your client.

2. Establish important reminders throughout the year to help you track trust funding reminders to grantors, premium due dates, Crummey notices, and policy review dates for each trust-owned life insurance policy.

3. Utilize a technology platform that supports trustees in monitoring policies' performance, deadlines, and needs. Most of them have automated calendar services and reminders to keep you on track. LifeTrust3D, LLC utilizes the industry's leading technology platform, *TOLI Vault*, created by industry innovator Mike Pepe.

4. Create annual policy reviews to share with your client. Remember: *annual policy <u>statements</u> from the insurance company alone do not provide enough information to understand how the policy is performing!* Even if they don't read the annual policy reviews, they will know their trustee is taking care of them.

5. Re-evaluate all goals of trust-owned policies at least every three years (or more often if recommended by the policy management statement). If clients aren't reading their annual policy reviews, be sure to make them slow down at least every three years for you to review it with them personally. This is the perfect time to revisit the "why" and understand what (if anything) has changed in the client's life.

7

How's Your Life Insurance Performing These Days?

IN OUR EXPERIENCE, roughly one third of trust-owned policies are left unmanaged. That means that, as with our friend Janet from chapter two, no one is monitoring them. We were fortunate with Janet, as her situation was relatively easy to resolve; there was plenty of cash value and she was in great health, so we simply needed to find a way to eliminate premium outlay. However, not all scenarios are this straightforward.

We've covered the four crucial questions to ask when assessing whether a client's policy is suiting their present needs, as well as the fiduciary issues that may arise from not having anyone in the pilot's seat; the next question to take into consideration should be, "How's your policy performing these days, anyway?" In terms of a policy's performance, the danger in not monitoring it lies in the fact that few really *know* if the policy is

Insurance decisions you might've made years ago are based on now out-of-date illustrations that likely projected significantly higher returns than the ones that are actually being received. A premature policy lapse or a large increase in premium funding can be avoided with a carefully engineered portfolio review that goes beyond simply reading annual statements.

meeting its expectations. Insurance companies mail statements, but statements alone do not even begin to constitute a thorough policy review.

Evolving developments in insurance products, pricing, and features, combined with any changes in your client's needs, all add up to the possibility that your client's life insurance plan—which we once thought of as secure—could now be inadequately funded and in jeopardy of lapse before a death benefit is paid. Insurance decisions you might've made years ago are based on now out-of-date illustrations that likely projected significantly higher returns than the ones that are actually being received. A premature policy lapse or a large increase in premium funding can be avoided with a carefully engineered portfolio review.

The 60s, 70s, 80s, and early 90s were times when most clients purchased insurance from agents selling "one size fits all" policies. There were fewer plan designs and policy types, which made the purchasing process much simpler. Today, the purchase of life insurance offers more choices in plan designs. A consumer now can—and should—purchase a policy specifically tailored to his or her individual goals. The early twenty-first century is characterized by increased compensation disclosure, fee transparency, and product choice as a result of the demand for a consumer-centric purchasing environment.

Policies today often fall short of original expectations for a number of reasons—lack of ongoing monitoring and service being the biggest one. If the initial design of the policy is poorly put together, chances are it won't last over time without re-engineering along the way. Remember the Chinese bamboo tree? The initial foundation needs to be strong before anything can flourish.

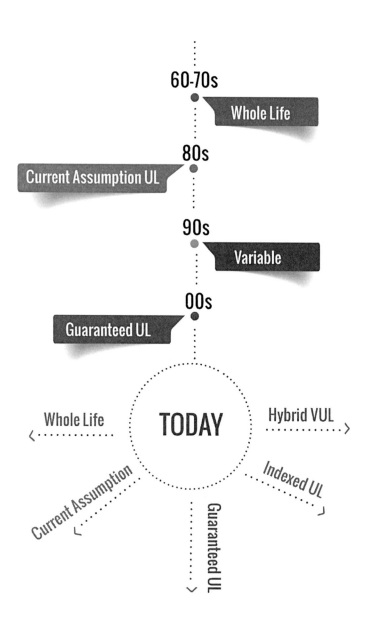

The Importance of Ongoing Policy Maintenance

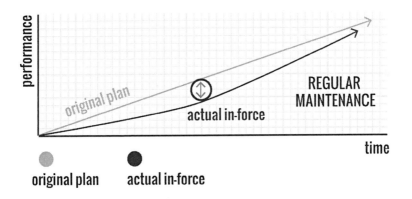

A well-managed policy doesn't necessarily mean the policy performs exactly as it was predicted to when sold. It means when the policy gets off course (as it most likely will), minor adjustments are made along the way in order to avoid what could amount to a much larger issue if left unattended.

Changes made by the insurance carrier in non-guaranteed elements—such as the dividend, the interest crediting rate, the cost of insurance, and more—also contribute to a policy not behaving as initially predicted, as well as a change in client need. It is crucial to bear in mind that change is constant, and with that general rule guiding life and all its details, management of any policy will take diligence.

In the low interest rate environment of 2015, product designs that are particularly at risk are Whole Life poli-

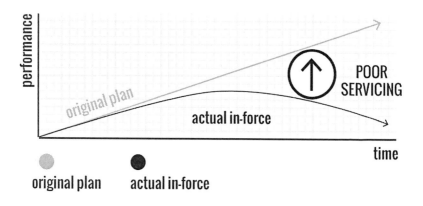

cies with significant "Term Riders" and Universal Life policies purchased in the 80s and 90s. The below is a graphic representation of how a Whole Life and Term Blend policy may have been explained to clients and sold when interest rates were higher than they are today.

ORIGINAL ILLUSTRATED MECHANICS

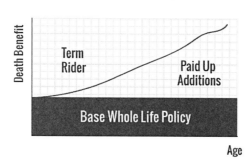

These graphics shows how the policies are actually performing within the low interest rate environment.

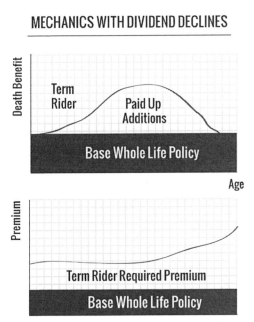

By monitoring and managing policies, we can start to ensure that we're achieving the results we're looking for. One way to create more positive consistency in your policy is to seek diversity in both policy type and insurance carrier. Diversification is particularly important for life insurance portfolios that generally have a death benefit greater than $3 million. Diversification among both insurance carriers and policy type is absolutely fundamental in designing those larger portfolios, and is described in more detail in section 3 of the Uniform Prudent Investor Act.

One way to create more positive consistency in your policy is to seek diversity in both policy type and insurance carrier. Diversification is particularly important for portfolios that generally have a death benefit greater than $3 million.

There are so many options in today's policy offerings (Universal Life, Variable, Whole Life, Index Universal Life, Hybrid Variable Universal Life … the list goes on) that you can diversify easily, taking care to find the *best* combination of policies. We were successful in re-engineering our client Janet's policy for a number of reasons, but what helped tremendously was the option to purchase two different policy types from two different carriers. Diversification may reduce risk and help clients cover all their bases; we can't know for certain what economic, political, or personal factors might impact a client's insurance portfolio in the future. If we maintain varying policies, we stand the best chance of protecting life insurance portfolios and adapting to future change.

Our economy's sustained low interest rate environment has forced dividend scales to continually decline. Companies that in 1988 yielded 10 percent dividends are now only crediting 5 or 6 percent dividends. As a result, premiums sometimes start to reappear just when a client thinks they've paid them all.[6]

A ninety-year-old named Gary was referred to me by a colleague. Convinced that his policy was fine as it was, Gary awoke one morning to a notice saying that his $1 million policy was going to lapse if he didn't come up with a $100,000 premium. The cash value was roughly $300,000 at that time. Gary had already paid in about $400,000 in premiums over fifteen years, and he was sure that he'd already entirely paid for the policy. He stated very clearly to me that he wouldn't give the insurance company "another dime of [his] money!" I knew immediately this was going to be a tough situation.

At Gary's age, the options were limited, and since he was still in great health, whatever plan we made couldn't be short-sighted. He wanted to surrender the policy for the $300,000 cash value. However, by working

---

6 Valmark Securities, http://www.LifeTrust3D, LLC.com/sites/default/files/ users/LifeTrust3D, LLC/HistoricalDividendScale2014.pdf

HISTORICAL DIVIDEND SCALES
Five AAA Rated Mutual Companies

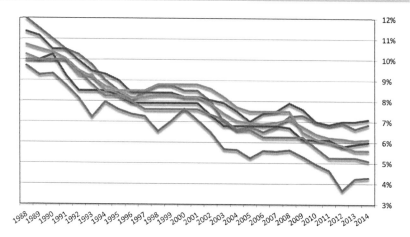

✔ The **average** Delta between Corporate Bond Yields and the 5 Mutual Companies illustrated here over the past 20 years has been **137 basis points.**

✔ **Currently**, the Delta between Corporate Yields and the average of the 5 Mutuals is at **184 basis points.**

- Guardian
- Massachusetts Mutual
- New York Life
- Northwestern Mutual
- Metropolitan Life
- AAA Corporate Yields*
- Mutuals' Average

While this graph is visually difficult to understand in grayscale (rather than color), the point is clear that in a low-interest environment you may find yourself in a situation where you are paying premiums longer than originally expected.

*AAA Yields taken from the Federal Reserve Bank of St. Louis, Economic Research-Average on monthly yields for the previous 12 months. Past results are not an indicator of future performance.

with his insurance carrier, we were able to "backdate" his reduced, paid-up death benefit options and secure a $580,000 death benefit. This allowed us to capture the maximum possible paid-up death benefit for Gary, and provided $280,000 more than if he had surrendered the policy. It wasn't the $1 million he had originally planned on, but it was much better than the alternative of a completely lapsed policy with no benefit at all. Sometimes we just have to make the best of a situation.

Unfortunately, Gary's situation is not unique. I dealt with a similar scenario for Mary, a ninety-three-year-old in excellent health. Mary had two $1 million life insurance policies, one of which was due to mature when she reached age ninety-five. In this case, "mature" meant the cash value at that time would be paid out to the beneficiaries. The cash value of that particular $1 million policy was projected to be $30,000 at age ninety-five—but now, at ninety-three, the cash value was $325,000. That meant that the annual cost of insurance was over $100,000 each year Mary lived, and if she lived to age ninety-five, her beneficiaries would only get $30,000! That didn't seem right to anyone.

After taking a closer look at Mary's situation, I saw that her second $1 million policy thankfully did not have a maturity age of ninety-five, like the other one.

However, if it was left underfunded, it would lapse when she turned ninety-five—but it would last much longer if she could contribute a higher premium. We completed an informal health assessment on Mary, and when it was clear that she maintained excellent health and could easily surpass age ninety-five, we made a tough recommendation to her trust officer: surrender her first policy now, while its cash value was still $300,000. The annual costs of insurance were exceeding $100,000 annually, and cash values were reducing by an average of $8,500 every month that passed. We then used that $300,000 to make sure her second policy was well-funded, and now, instead of lapsing at age ninety-five, that $1 million policy will stay in force until Mary reaches the age of *one hundred* and five.

At first blush, one might argue that surrendering a $1 million life insurance policy on a ninety-three-year-old's life was poor planning. If Mary were to die suddenly, the decisions made would surely be questioned. However, once we'd documented the file appropriately and collaborated with the family and their advisors, we agreed that sacrificing one policy to save another was best in that situation. If Mary were to stay alive past age ninety-five, these policies that she'd been putting money into for years would have suddenly meant nothing. By making an informed and educated decision, we were able to breathe life back into one of the policies that could then provide a $1 million benefit for her family.

There are so many times when we have very difficult choices to face. We learn from both Gary and Mary that some life insurance policies sold years ago may not have been structured to stand the test of time and insureds living into their late nineties. In both cases, if these issues had been addressed earlier, a more favorable outcome for their families might have been possible. I am hopeful that with more trustees proactively pursuing policy reviews, fewer and fewer clients will have to face the challenges that Gary and Mary faced.

With people now living longer and older policies not necessarily designed for longevity into the late nineties, many trust officers will find themselves with clients like Gary and Mary. Advisors like us support not only clients, but trustees as well—many don't necessarily have the expertise and knowledge to make these kinds of tough decisions. We help facilitate these conversations and ferret out all possibilities to provide options and help make the *best* decisions, even if it means sacrificing one policy to save another.

In consistently monitoring policies, it will become easier to know what decisions to make and when, or at least when to ask for help. Think of it, again, as maintenance of the Chinese bamboo: if you don't check on the soil routinely, how will you know that your plant needs water? Vigilance is the first crucial step in cultivating *the best policy*.

8

Why Free Insurance Advice is Worth What You Pay for It (That Would Be Nothing, if You Do the Math)

IMAGINE THAT YOU have decided to build a house for yourself. You're not an architect, you're not a construction expert, you're not a plumber or an electrician, but you love your ideas and want to abide by them to some degree. Chances are that the first step you'd take would be to hire a professional who has the expertise to bring your ideas to life—and do it well. You could certainly wire the house yourself, but if you don't know the first thing about electricity, and you might put yourself and your family in danger by doing it without an expert's guidance.

Most contractors receive the completion of their payment after they've completed the work. It's a practical concept for the consumer and motivation for the worker; if your contractors don't do their jobs well (or even finish their jobs), why would you want to pay them?

In financial management, the principle is the same. Advisors are paid for their expertise, knowledge base, and ability—for their intellectual assets. Charging fees for life insurance policy management is new territory for many. "I've already paid my agent to help me," a client might think, "and since my policy is still in effect, I should be able to get free advice from the agent or insurance carrier … right?"

The issue with the insurance industry is that agents are paid the majority of their compensation upon completion of the sale, and there is minimal obligation to service policies regularly. The best agents understand policy service is vital to their ongoing relationships with their valued clients. However, not all policyholders and trustees experience proactive policy reviews.

Today, free insurance reviews are now being offered throughout the country. The word "free" always sucks people in, and why shouldn't it? But those reviews are being offered because the companies want to get clients in the door. It's worth everything to the salespeople looking for policy exchanges—and not much to a client looking for unbiased advice. Our experience shows that policy exchanges may make sense in approximately

25 percent of reviews, but what about the other 75 percent of the time, where a policy modification or simply leaving the current policy in its current state is the right answer?

At LifeTrust3D, LLC, we manage insurance for a family office whose total death benefit is hundreds of millions of dollars. Within the multiple trusts, ten different individuals are insured with sixty different poli-

In the insurance industry, most agents are paid the majority of their compensation upon completion of the sale, and there is minimal obligation to service policies regularly. The best agents understand that policy service is vital to their ongoing relationships with their valued clients.

cies issued by nine insurance companies. These policies were sold to the family by six different insurance agents over the course of thirty years. That's ten people, sixty policies, nine companies, six insurance agents, and thirty years. Tired yet? Imagine being the CFO of this family office and trying to manage all of those policies!

With an insurance portfolio of such magnitude, a family may consider hiring a third-party review firm specializing in life insurance policy management and monitoring on a fee basis. A CFO for a family office doesn't have time to meet with six different insurance agents for consultation and typically doesn't even want to; they'd give six different answers, and chances are their recommendations would have a lot to do with purchasing or adding new policies. (You know the old insurance joke: if you are on a plane and don't want the person next to you to talk, just tell them you sell life insurance for a living. I guarantee a silent ride!)

A fee-based insurance advisor is paid for his or her expertise. The founders of LifeTrust3D, LLC started charging fees to manage significant life insurance portfolios over fifteen years ago. We came to understand that there is indeed a niche market for people like us. Fee-based insurance advisors can be more objective when it comes to managing clients' portfolios, and since we are working on a fee basis, we don't have to sell them anything new to be fairly compensated for our work. Rather, we are there to look out for their best interest. Fee-based operations support clients in finding *the best policy*—the one that is right for them. The answer can't always be "buy a replacement policy," and a client trusts an advisor to find the right answer. Like the Chinese bamboo, a trust-owned life insurance policy or any significant insurance portfolio needs consistent nourishment and care over time in order to reach its full potential. If there's no advisor properly assisting a client, how can a policy flourish?

In today's world, there are not a lot of qualified advisors helping to support trustees in managing policies. Most experienced insurance agents are retiring. For clients, the opportunity for insurance replacement has decreased dramatically. In 2012, 42 percent of the policies we reviewed had replacement opportunities, but only about 36 percent did in 2013. For 2014, we estimate that roughly 31 percent of policies will require a replacement to improve the client's situation—a consistent and important decrease. Modification is our primary recommendation to date, meaning that the number of policies we manage that are simply modified or restructured with the current carrier is growing consistently.

One of the qualities I most admired about my father was his unwillingness to jeopardize a client's well-being for the sake of making a dollar. I know he learned this from his mentor, the late Henry Colton, and I'm grateful that he passed that value on to me. I'm even more grateful that he provided financial stability for us so that both he and I could operate that way. Being provided for as a kid and having that foundation as an adult liberated me

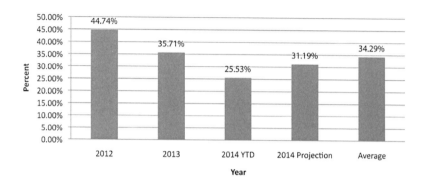

PERCENT OF POLICY REVIEWS RESULTING IN REPLACEMENT
(REPRESENTATIVE OF COLTON GROOME & COMPANY CASES ONLY)

to act from a place of social and ethical consciousness, rather than acting from a place of need or greed. Selling is not inherently bad—it just needs to be done at the right time, under the right circumstances. Getting paid for your expertise is the most rewarding position to be in!

Going forward, we envision a world in which, once a policy is purchased, ongoing policy management is part of the "sale" and commitment to the client. When we charge fees for our consulting services at LifeTrust3D, LLC, expert insurance advisors are paid for their thoughts and ideas, which are delivered through the industry's leading technology platform.

Creating my own firm was a crowning achievement for me. It enabled to me to utilize the values that I hold dear in order to better serve trustees, fiduciaries, and clients. Many people shudder when they hear the term *life insurance*. I want that stigma to go away. I want people to be able to open a statement without panicking; to be able to call an advisor for help without pressure. I want people to love life insurance again.

Life insurance, though complex, does something that no other financial tool in the world can do: it can provide financially for a wealth creator's family, charitable intentions, estate, and legacy when that wealth creator is no longer here to do so. Our philosophy at LifeTrust3D, LLC is that every policy receives its due diligence, year after year, regardless of policy type (Term, Whole Life, Variable Life, Universal Life, Indexed Life, hybrids, etc.). We are relentless about working toward and ensuring the best possible outcomes for all the policies that we are fortunate enough to manage.

I think often of my client Charles, and of Guy and Janet and Gary, and I know that I want to be the kind of advisor who is known for giving the right answer—the advisor people call when they want an answer that isn't self-serving, but rather in the best interest of the client. That is why LifeTrust3D, LLC was born.

9

Designing Your Insurance Plan in Today's Environment

POTENTIAL GRANTORS ARE likely interested in available policies and pricing, and yet may not know whom to turn to for preliminary discussions with family or advisors. The purpose of this chapter is to provide trustees, attorneys, accountants, and other professionals a foundation on which to build a meaningful life insurance conversation. Your clients will need an expert to assist not only with the selection of *the best policy*, but with the monitoring and management of that policy.

When shopping for new life insurance in a consumer-driven market, the first question everyone asks is, "How much does life insurance cost?" Any true insurance professional would prefer to begin the dialogue somewhere other than price, but it is inevitably the first question—especially as it relates to trust-owned life insurance. The chart below will provide a response to clients, with the expectation that the next question will be, "Well, which one is best for my situation?"

Sample Policy Pricing for $1,000,000

"Which one is best for me?" is the exact question we want to hear. This is where an expert insurance advisor employs his or her expertise, listening skills, and knowledge—three of the many ways in which we differentiate ourselves from a highly commoditized industry. The chart below provides a simple explanation outlining the advantages and disadvantages of different life insurance policy types.

Expert insurance advisors should utilize a preliminary questionnaire to better understand the client's goals and appropriately match the most suitable policy type to their circumstances. It also allows us to document the purpose for life insurance through a Policy Management Statement and justify the policy type selected for the trustee. Knowing that there is no "one-size-fits-all" insurance plan and that every policy type has advantages and disadvantages, we emphasize three critical factors in the policy selection process. These three selection criteria, along with medical underwriting, will have the most significant impact in answering the client's first question, "How much does life insurance cost?"

MALE - PREFERRED NONSMOKER

Product			Age 45		Age 55		Age 65	
	Low	High	Low	High	Low	High	Low	High
10 YT	$800	$1,600	$2,000	$3,100	$5,300	$8,300	$17,600	$22,700
20 YT	$1,400	$2,200	$3,500	$5,300	$11,500	$13,800	-	-
30 YT	$2,300	$4,600	$6,800	$7,400	-	-	-	-
GUL	$7,100	$11,600	$11,500	$14,300	$20,500	$28,700	$39,400	$53,300
HVUL	$8,900	$13,300	$14,500	$22,200	$24,400	$37,200	$44,700	$67,600
HUL	$6,700	$7,500	$11,200	$11,700	$19,300	$19,900	$33,700	$39,000
WL	$15,300	$18,800	$22,700	$32,600	$39,100	$61,400	$63,600	$109,400
CAUL	$6,700	$12,000	$11,100	$19,700	$19,300	$33,000	$36,000	$57,800
CAUL7	$29,200	$50,600	$43,100	$65,700	$67,400	$87,300	$101,400	$119,500

FEMALE - PREFERRED NONSMOKER

Product			Age 45		Age 55		Age 65	
	Low	High	Low	High	Low	High	Low	High
10 YT	$700	$1,400	$1,400	$2,400	$3,200	$5,200	$11,300	$16,700
20 YT	$1,000	$1,500	$2,400	$3,500	$6,500	$9,500	-	-
30 YT	$1,800	$2,300	$4,500	$6,500	-	-	-	-
GUL	$5,600	$9,100	$9,700	$13,000	$16,500	$23,100	$30,300	$42,900
HVUL	$7,400	$10,800	$11,400	$17,800	$20,700	$34,400	$38,900	$55,000
HUL	$5,600	$6,000	$9,100	$9,600	$15,800	$16,200	$28,700	$32,500
WL	$13,000	$17,000	$19,200	$28,200	$31,100	$50,900	$53,200	$95,400
CAUL	$5,600	$10,100	$9,600	$16,200	$16,200	$26,600	$30,000	$45,800
CAUL7	$25,500	$45,600	$38,800	$59,400	$56,600	$79,900	$90,100	$108,200

YT - Year Term; **GUL** - Guaranteed Universal Life; **HVUL** - Hybrid Variable Universal Life; **HUL** - Hybrid Universal Life; **WL** - Whole Life; **CAU** - Current Assumption UL; **CAUL7** - Current Assumption UL (7-Pay)

WHAT CAN IMPACT THE FUNDING LEVEL?

- A change in risk class from Preferred Nonsmoker to Standard Nonsmoker could increase required premiums by **23%**
- Adding a Waiver of Premium Rider could increase required premiums by **9%**
- Adding a LTC Rider could increase required premiums by **11%**
- Reducing the guarantee length to age 100 could decrease required premiums by **7%**

NOTES: Figures last updated July 2013. Figures presented are based on carrier averages. Percentage changes are based on guaranteed universal life policies. Any hypothetical investment performance data contained within this document are included for illustrative and purposes only, not as a representative of past or future results. Actual results will vary from those illustrated.

WHOLE LIFE — LIFE INSURANCE PRODUCT OVERVIEW

ADVANTAGES	DISADVANTAGES
Guaranteed premiums – cannot change	Expensive – highest premium for the death benefit
Fully reserved with cash values available to policy owners	Inflexible design – difficult to change premium or death benefit
Over 100+ years history. Whole life has consistently paid benefits	Actual dividends are unlikely to be as high as currently illustrated dividend crediting rates
	Dividends paid at insurance company's discretion and based upon fixed income returns only.

UNIVERSAL LIFE **WITHOUT** SECONDARY DEATH BENEFIT GUARANTEES

ADVANTAGES	DISADVANTAGES
Lower projected premium	Client at risk for having to pay higher premium
A great amount of premium flexibility	Company can change cost of insurance, credited rate and expense charges
Adjustable death benefit	Very little is guaranteed - Almost everything is subject to company's discretion

UNIVERSAL LIFE **WITH** SECONDARY DEATH BENEFIT GUARANTEES

ADVANTAGES	DISADVANTAGES
Lowest guaranteed premium	Very high expense loads lead to low cash values
Guaranteed Premiums – cannot change	Analysts, academics and regulators are concerned that the inability to adjust charges may create financial pressure on the company.
Premiums remain flexible. However, changes in premiums may adversely affect guarantees.	The "worst case" is also the "best case". No potential for better-than-guaranteed results. Little or no ability to adapt policy to future changes.
	If not properly managed, guarantees can be lost, leading to expensive "catch-ups" or policy lapse.

VARIABLE UNIVERSAL LIFE **WITHOUT** DEATH BENEFITS GUARANTEES

ADVANTAGES	DISADVANTAGES
All expenses are described in prospectus. The client controls investment	Client has a higher premium if targeted returns are not achieved as illustrated
Historically higher rates of return can be used to reduce premium payments, increase benefits or provide flexibility	Volatility of returns affects policy performance.
Additional safety of separate accounts give maximum protection from insurance company insolvency	Some clients are not sophisticated enough to understand or manage product
	Product may not be suitable for very conservative policyholders

VARIABLE UNIVERSAL LIFE **WITH** DEATH BENEFITS GUARANTEES

All advantages of Variable Universal Life	These products have charges for the guarantees. Younger clients with robustly funded VUL policies may prefer lower charges of VUL.
All advantages of Universal Life with Secondary Death Benefit Guarantees.	Guaranteed premiums are higher than with Non- Variable Universal Life. The upside potential may not offset this for older age clients.
Combines flexibility, low overall cost and potential for strong performance	Fewer insurance companies offer this product.

1. **Certainty:** the degree of confidence one has that the policy design parameters will perform as expected. This may include non-guaranteed factors such as the insurance carrier's dividend rate for Whole Life policies, the interest-crediting rate on a Universal Life policy, or earnings rate assumption on a Variable or Indexed Universal Life policy. Every illustration has a disclaimer stating, "This is a life insurance illustration and not a contract. Actual results may vary from the illustrated values shown in in this illustration." There are factors the insurance carrier controls and factors the policy owner controls, all of which are subject to change.

2. **Safety:** the degree of protection afforded to your plan. Safety is measured by the financial strength of the chosen life insurance carrier and by the secondary premium and death benefit guarantees included in the life insurance contract. Guarantees, backed by the claims-paying ability of the insurance carrier,

may provide comforting assurance that the premium and/or death benefit is guaranteed to average life expectancy, or age 100, or for an insured's lifetime. In the life insurance environment of 2015, the longer the guarantee, the higher the premium.

3. **Equity:** the ability of a policy to build cash value over time. Generally, policies that build cash value may require greater premium outlay than those that don't, but they often provide more flexibility in the event that the needs or goals of the trust change in the future.

Certainty, safety and equity play a significant role in designing *the best policy*. Oftentimes, we have to help clients prioritize which components are most important in building their best policy. Designing the plan is only the beginning. You must have a qualified life insurance professional who can carry out the plan and nourish it until it blossoms. Choose your professional carefully, as he or she is likely the most important part of the process.

10

The Best Policy

"SO WHAT IS '*the best policy*,' anyway?" asked John, my newest client. John, a young and successful surgeon, had been referred to me after an estate planning review with his attorney. John had been sold a policy a few years ago by another agent and had come into my office to get a fresh perspective, frustrated with his policy's performance in comparison to what originally had been promised.

The first thing out of his mouth had been, "Thanks for meeting with me. I'm concerned I was sold a bill of goods, and now I don't understand my policy. I thought it was the best policy for me, but now I'm not so sure. The agent who sold it to me was my father's friend, but he's now retired, and I don't know where else to turn."

"Well, John," I said, "I can't perform surgery, so it's unfair to ask *you* to understand all the ins and outs of life insurance. What I *am* able to do is help you better understand your current life insurance policy and evaluate your options. Then, once we agree on the appropriate path forward, our firm will assist you in monitoring and managing the plan so you don't get off course again. How does that sound?"

John looked at me blankly and said, "You mean you're not going to try to sell me something?"

With a big smile on my face, I joked, "I wouldn't go that far now," and we laughed together.

"Think of it this way," I said to him. "Why did you purchase the policy initially? Is that reason still relevant?"

It turned out that John was disappointed in the policy's cash value accumulation and felt like it wasn't performing as well as he had originally been told it would. The cash value accumulation was secondary, though. His primary motivation for purchasing life insurance was to provide a substantial death benefit to his wife and two young children should he pass away before them.

John and I talked for almost an hour about his goals and hopes for his policy, and how they might have changed even over a short-term horizon. In John's situation, we were able to confirm that the policy he'd originally purchased was indeed the best one for him based on him completing our trademarked process, which included a policy benchmarking study of his policy compared to alternatives available in today's life insurance marketplace. Creating *the best policy* for John, as it turned out, meant the same thing it means for approximately 75 percent of the policies we review: making a slight modification to the policy in order to improve its performance and meet the needs of John's family.

Life insurance is a curiously personalized beast. My role with John was simply to listen, assess the situation, and provide an objective framework for him to make an educated and informed decision. Based on the information we had already gathered before John came in, I had a notion that maintaining his current policy would provide the *best* outcome for John. However, it was important for him to be part of the process, and understand it for himself. My goal was for him to have greater confidence in his life insurance policy ... and maybe even love it again. Well, maybe he wouldn't love the policy itself, but I thought perhaps he would love and appreciate the protection and security it could provide for the ones he loved most in this world.

There's no "one size fits all" with life insurance. We fully recognize that the purchase of a policy is only the beginning. Change is inevitable. Political and economic factors constantly affect policies and their purpose in a plan. Estate tax laws, insurance carrier strength, the health of the insured, the policy's performance, the grantor's ability to gift funds to the trust—these are all influencing factors that are in constant flux. Assess and reassess the goals and performance of your clients' life insurance portfolios in the face of an ever-changing world, and in doing so, you'll have taken the most crucial step in ensuring that the policy supports your client's needs and goals.

As you make adjustments to policies to meet clients' needs within these changes, each adjustment needs to be deliberate and well documented. It's the same reason we monitor policies annually rather than simply accepting an annual policy *statement*: the devil is in the details, and when a choice that isn't backed by careful thought is put into play, those details can be overlooked and cause problems down the line. When people purchase these policies, they're not just purchasing a product or purchasing a policy for themselves. They're purchasing a promise that their policy will serve them and the ones they love most today and into the future. We want them to be able to see the fruits of that promise. During that meeting, John was sold something after all—not a product, but a *promise* that LifeTrust3D, LLC would commit to managing and monitoring his life insurance policy annually on a fee basis. I smiled at him and said, "See, I told you I might sell you something."

John replied, much more seriously than I'd anticipated, "No, Tate, you didn't sell me. I knew our family needed your help, and my attorney told me you would take good care of us. I want to work with your firm, and will happily do so. Your fee reflects that value you will be providing to us."

We shook hands, and I prepared to see him out of the office. Before we got to the door, though, he stopped me.

"Wait," he said. "You never told me what 'the best policy' is!"

I smiled. "Actually, John, I've been telling you all along. *The best policy* is the one that's right for *you!*"

After John left my office, I sat silently for a bit. I couldn't help but think of myself years before, as fresh-faced as John, and yet somehow listening to one of the wealthiest men in our community tell me about his hopes and fears. Charles. He'd trusted me, and together, we'd made decisions that had worked. He purchased a promise from me, and I was able to see it through. That promise has impacted every policy I've sold or managed since. I thought of Henry Colton and the values he'd instilled in my father, who so graciously passed them to me and my brother. I thought of the $100,000 trust distribution Guy and I were able to negotiate with the trustee that hit his three daughters' personal bank accounts that Christmas Eve a few years earlier. I thought of all my younger clients with young families they love and want to protect. That meeting with John was a culmination of many stories and experiences for me. When John and I shook hands at the end of our meeting, the sermon I'd heard just the Sunday before hit me like a ton of bricks.

The Chinese bamboo needs careful attention and nourishment to establish a secure and intricate root system. Crafting this foundation requires a significant investment of time, energy, and a little love—but if you can dedicate yourself to that investment, your bamboo will flourish. You'll have a healthy entity that can support itself as long as you provide it with whatever it needs, be it fertilizer, water, or protection from the weather.

The same is true of trust-owned life insurance. Only with the appropriate attention and nourishment can it flourish. Clients need a trust that they can indeed *trust*, and in order to get that, they need a team of advisors and a life insurance policy they can trust as well. The path to a trustworthy life insurance portfolio? Creating and nourishing that *best policy, the one created specifically for you, managed consistently for you, while always being mindful that it's not necessarily for you—but for those you love.*

Acknowledgments

I AM WHERE I am today because of my faith, family, and friends.

First, I give thanks to God, who is good.

To Anna, my wife: you are the most amazing and beautiful woman I have ever known, and I still have to pinch myself to believe that I wasn't dreaming when you said yes. Thank you for always supporting me, loving me, and believing in me (even when I didn't). I cherish you and every second of our journey together.

To my wonderful children, Davis, Lillian, and Evan: You bring out the best in me, and I want to make you proud. You have taught me and your mom the true meaning of love. Lillian and Evan, you both have been incredible fighters in your little lives, and proven that you are survivors. You are my superheroes. Davis, being the oldest isn't always easy, but you represent all that is good in this world. God has blessed the three of you with incredible gifts; share them graciously and stay faithful.

The Groome brothers: If I am ever in a foxhole, I'd want my father, George (who introduces himself to secretaries as my older brother when out on appointments!) and my brother, Matt, right in there with me. Getting to work with my two best friends doesn't even seem fair. I would put the three of us up against anyone. Dad, thank you for teaching me the business and investing in me. I may not have a Master's degree, but I have the only Ph.D. from the George Groome School of Business (and Life) in the entire country! This book is dedicated to you. It is amazing what you have created and how many lives you have touched along the way. Matt and I are so fortunate to have a teacher, mentor, friend, and father in you. Matt, bro, I can't believe how far you have come in such a short time in this business. You are the guy I want next to me in business and in life. You are my best friend and I don't tell you enough, but I love you.

Mom: thanks for saying yes on the day in May 2003 when I called Dad asking if I could come work with him. (Remember—he had to call me back that night so he could go home and ask your permission?) You are the glue that holds our family together, and the best person I know. Thank you for loving all of us as you do. You are truly an angel.

To the late Henry Colton: You taught my father so much that is now ingrained in me. You had the best sense of humor, but my favorite line of yours will always be, "Don't say 'Boo-Boo' when just 'Boo' will do."

To the Colton Family: thank you for taking my dad into your home. Not a day goes by that he doesn't pay homage to Henry and your family. When a new client comes into Colton Groome & Company, we always open with: "Colton Groome & Company was founded on October 1st, 1950 by Henry Colton. Henry was educated as an engineer at Yale, flew over twenty combat missions during WWII, survived, and came back to make the law review and the University of North Carolina at Chapel Hill. When you combine the precision of an engineer, the courage of a WWII combat aviator, and the thoroughness of an attorney, that is the fabric and foundation upon which our firm was built." I can't tell you how many times I leaned on Henry's legacy in our community when I first came into the industry as a young man. We will be forever grateful to the Coltons.

To the local attorneys, national bank trust officers, and community bankers who have entrusted your most precious client relationships to me and our firm: Thank you. You are the reason we created LifeTrust3D, LLC, and the reason I wrote this book. I am grateful to call you all my friends and colleagues.

To my clients: without your trust and confidence, none of this would be possible. Some of you have known me since I was in diapers; some of you I grew up with; some of you I've met as an adult; and many of you are spread across the U.S. and we've never met personally. However, your stories, families, and lives touch mine every day. I am forever thankful for all of you.

Finally, I have been fortunate to cross paths with three people and one organization that have had a tremendous impact in my professional career:

Larry J. Rybka: as the leader of Valmark Securities, you have freely shared your time over the last ten years helping a young guy like me come up in this crazy business we call life insurance. Although you support hundreds of producers nationwide, I always feel like you have time for me, and that you have a special interest in my success. You lead by doing things the right way with Christian principles; it is easy to follow a leader like you.

Valmark Securities, Inc.: You are more than a broker-dealer; you are like family. A special thanks to Tom Love for his work on Chapter 5. Also, the diagrams, charts, and graphics are all from Valmark Securities, Inc. I thank you for sharing your expertise and always challenging your advisors to be our best. Moving our broker-dealer to Valmark was the single most impactful business decision Colton Groome & Company ever made. Thank you for being exceptional.

Mike Pepe: from Pizza to Life Insurance ... to Technology. Who would have thought that happenstance meeting at the bar far away from both of our homes would have turned into this? I cannot believe what you have created with the TOLI Vault™—it is, hands down, the *best* ILIT administration platform in our business. I am so proud of what you have accomplished, and proud to call you my friend.

Robert Berman: yes, I saved you for last! Man, you gave me the confidence to pull all of this off. I can't believe how far we have come. Thanks for pushing me and believing in me. You are incredibly talented, and I admire your ability to just get things done. That is uncommon today in the business development world, but you make it seem simple. I am so grateful to have you on my team.

More About the Author

G. Tate Groome is the founder and driving force behind LifeTrust3D™, LLC, and the motivation and heart behind finding ...*the Best Policy*. A Certified Financial Planner™ and Chartered Life Underwriter™, he has over a decade of experience in providing trusted life insurance solutions to individuals, trustees, and advisors. He recently won the distinguished "40 under 40 Award" in Asheville, NC, and is a recipient of the North Carolina Volunteer Award, chosen by the governor of NC. He earned his degree from UNC Chapel Hill.

Prior to forming LifeTrust3D™, LLC, Tate taught elementary education and coached basketball for at-risk youth. He then began working for Colton Groome & Company, where he is now a principal. He is a member of the Top of the Table and Million Dollar Roundtable®, as well as the local NAIFA committee. Tate serves on several boards: the YMCA of Western North Carolina, South Buncombe Youth Basketball, and Skyland United Methodist Church. He also coaches the basketball, soccer, and baseball teams on which his three children play. Tate is happily married, and he and his family live in Asheville, NC.

Tate is available to speak at conferences, seminars, trade shows, association meetings, and corporate events. LifeTrust3D™, LLC also offers certified continuing education classes (in person and online) for trustees, attorneys, and CPAs. **To contact Tate and LifeTrust3D™, LLC for seminars, speaking engagements, classes, and more:**

G. Tate Groome, CFP®, CLU®
Managing Partner, LifeTrust3D™, LLC
Toll-free: 844-747-5833 (*THIS IS LT3D*)
Fax: 828-254-5895
1127-B Hendersonville Road
Asheville, NC 28803
www.LifeTrust3D.com
www.tategroome.com